FLOWER PATTERN COLORING PAGES VOLUME 1

I0482691

Floral Patterns Coloring Book Pages

RICHARD EDWARD HARGREAVES

PUBLISHER'S NOTE

The creation of the 50 floral patterns in this book have been inspired by nature and derived from floral motifs, plinths, and mandalas.

The detailed interlocking repeating patterns range from moderate to very intricate, and are best suited for intermediate to advanced level colorists. Most are quite challenging in the degree of detail and intricacy, and will provide hours of rewarding coloring enjoyment and pleasure. The designs combine the beauty of nature with the hypnotic appeal of mandalas and tile patterns. These inspiring works of art are designed to stimulate the imaginations of colorists. The detailed line images offer a wealth of variety and the coloring possibilities are endless. We hope you enjoy them as much as we are thrilled to present them to you.

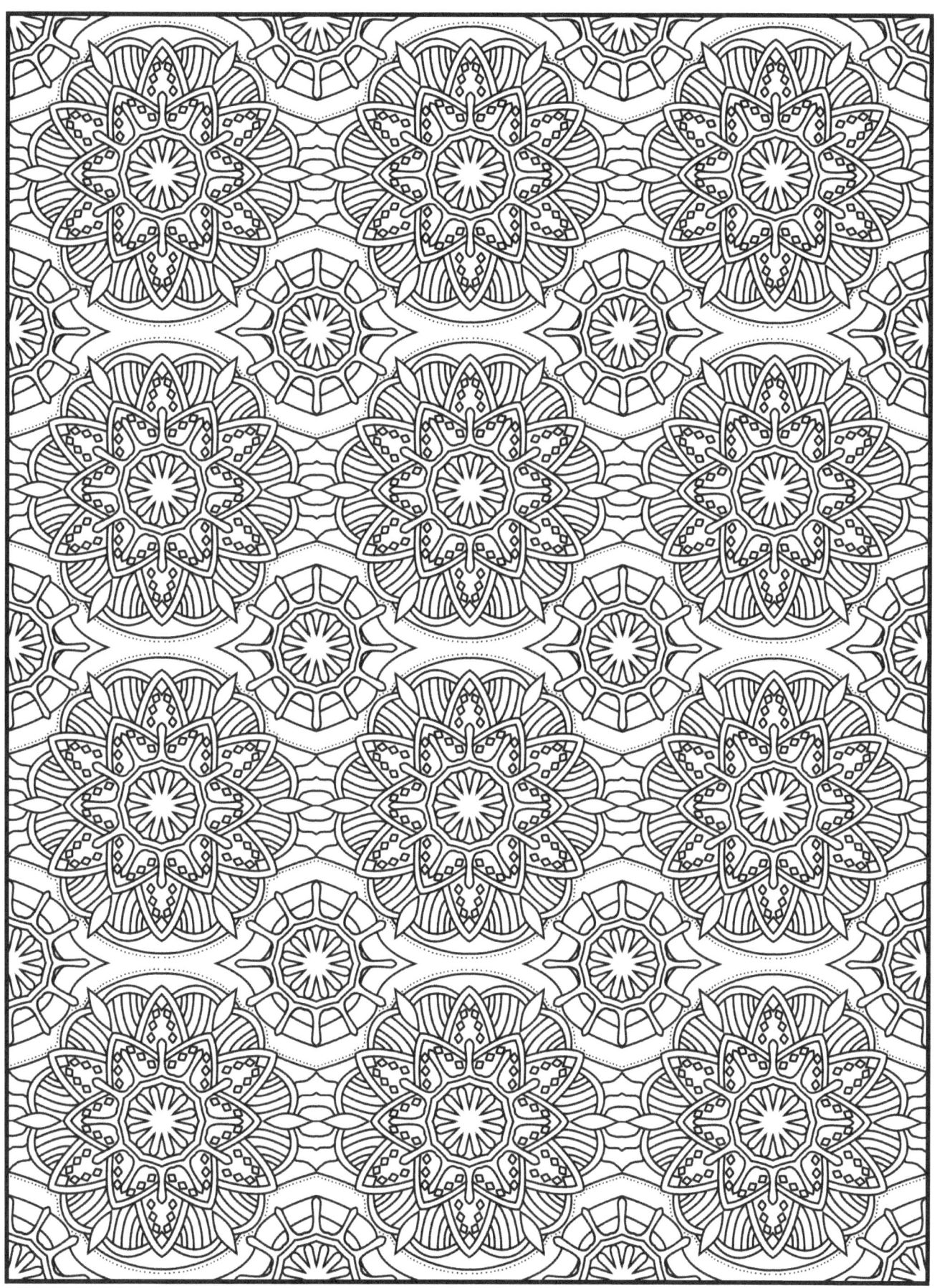

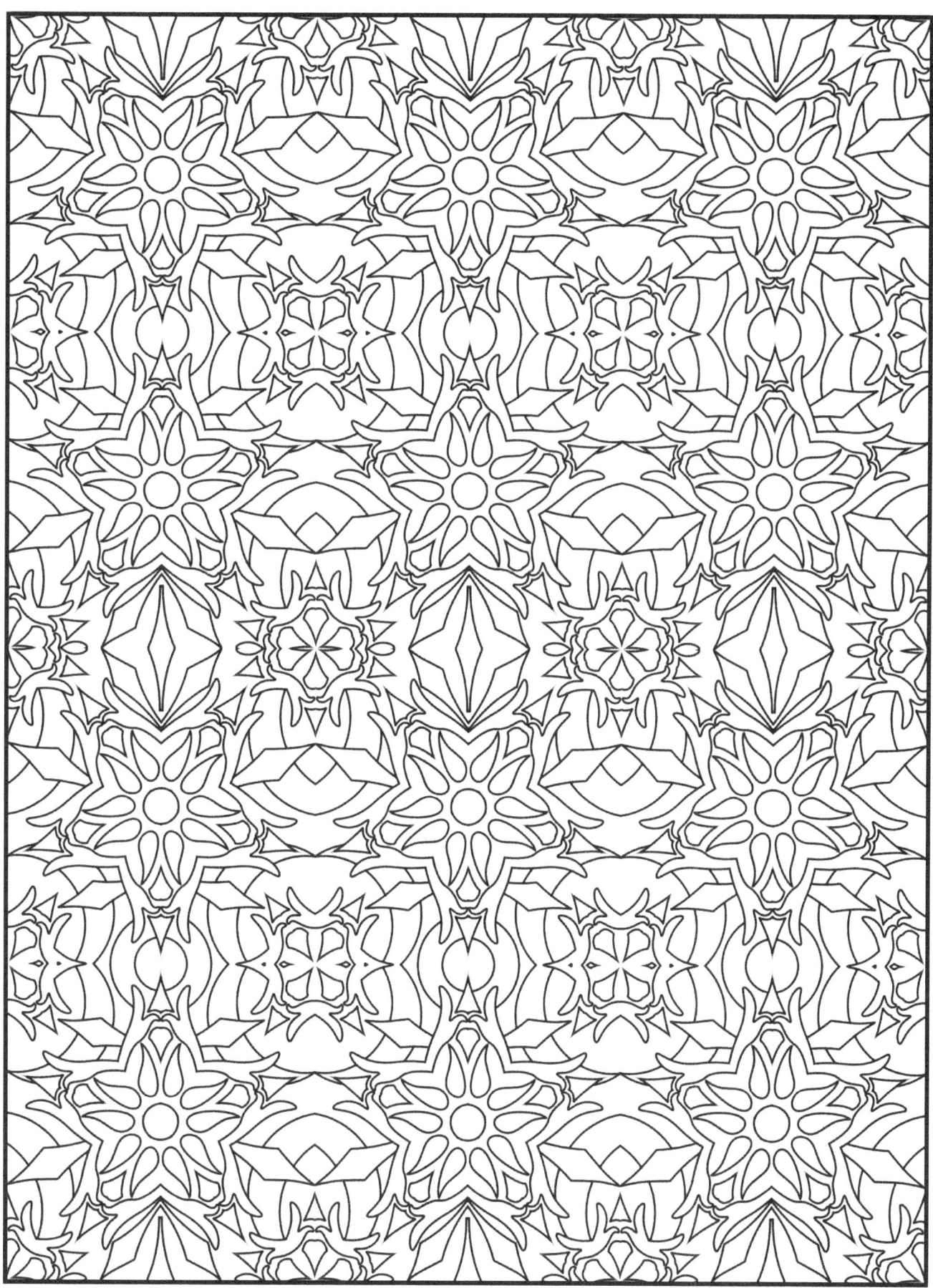

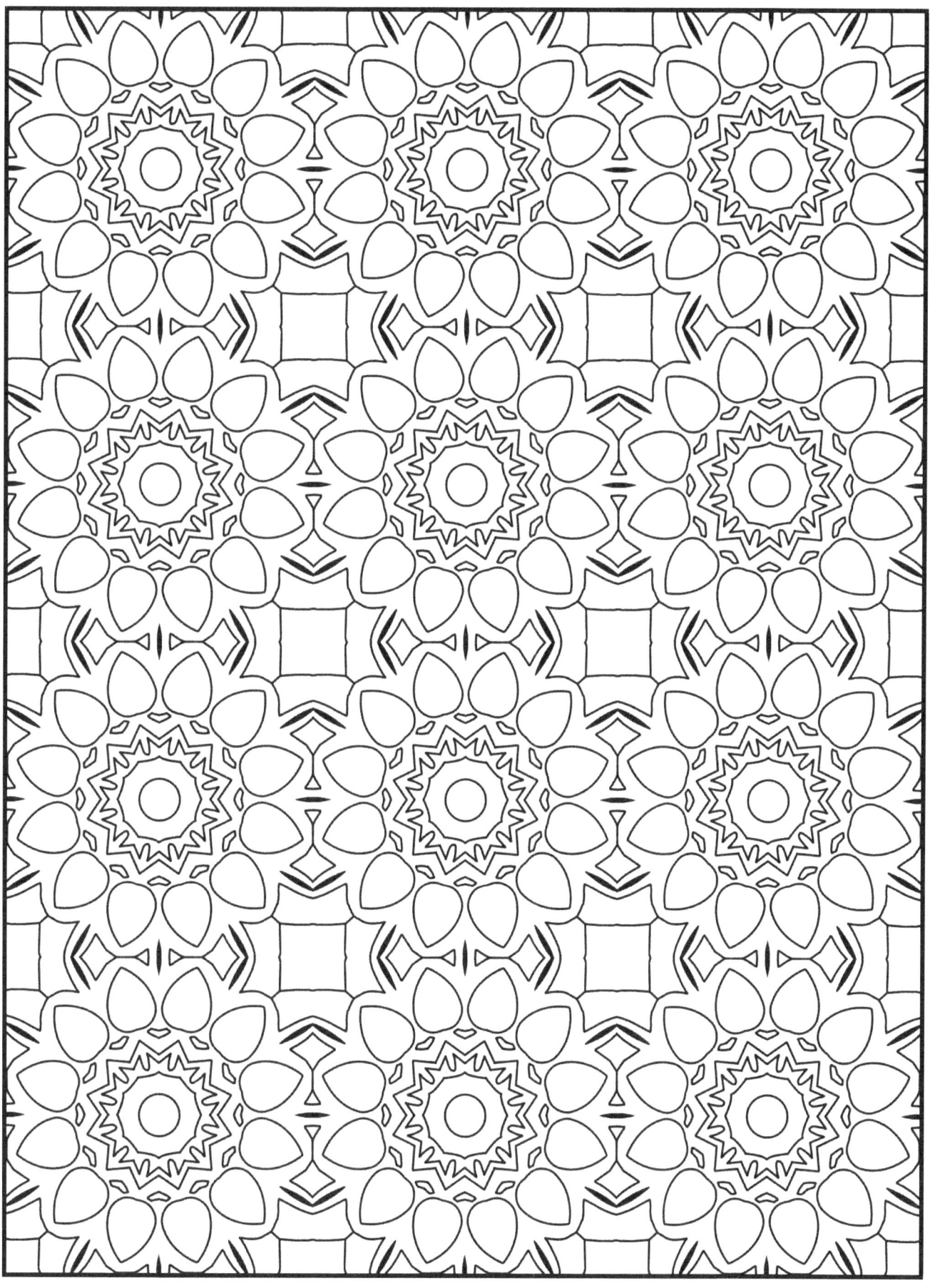

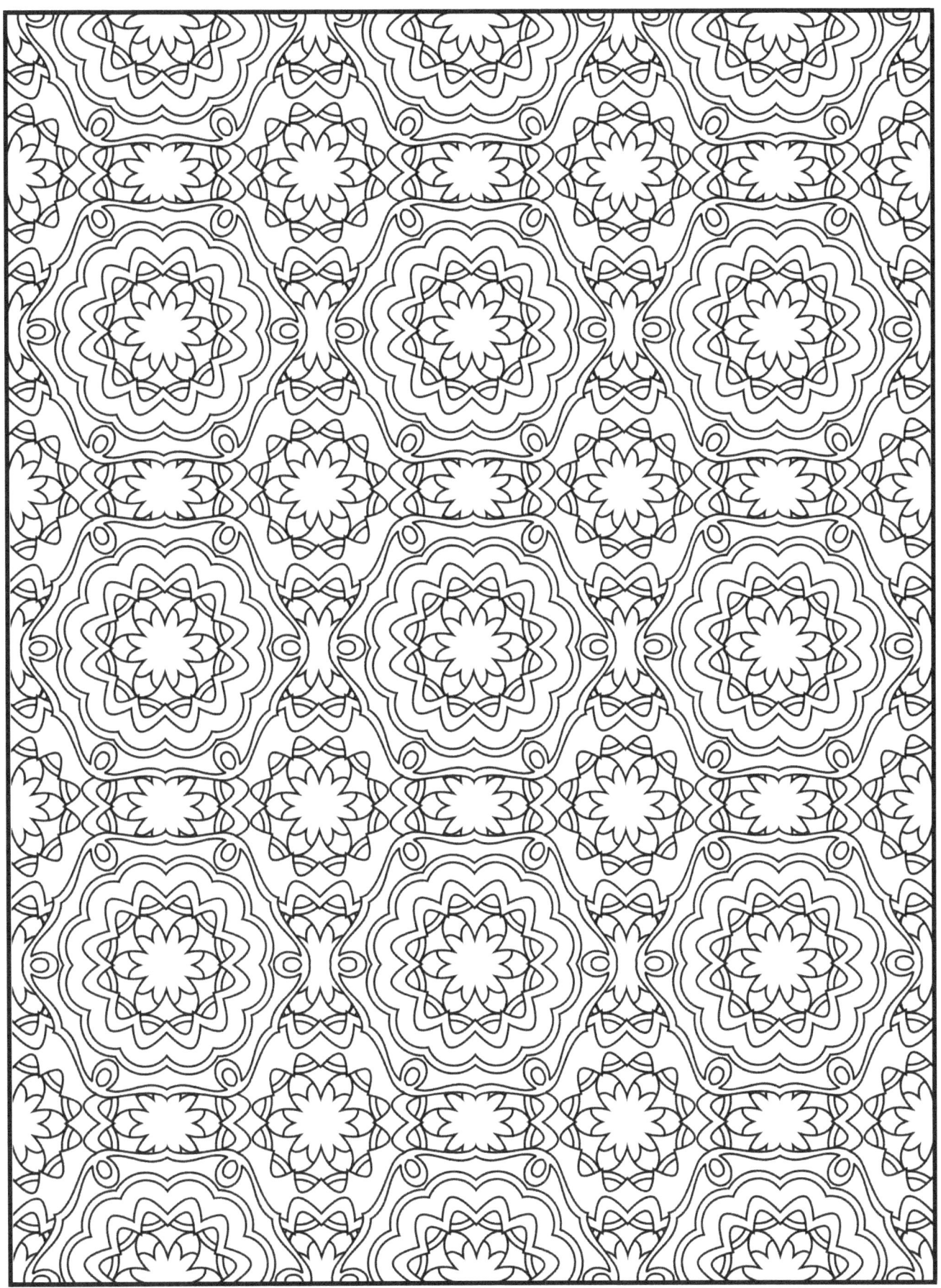

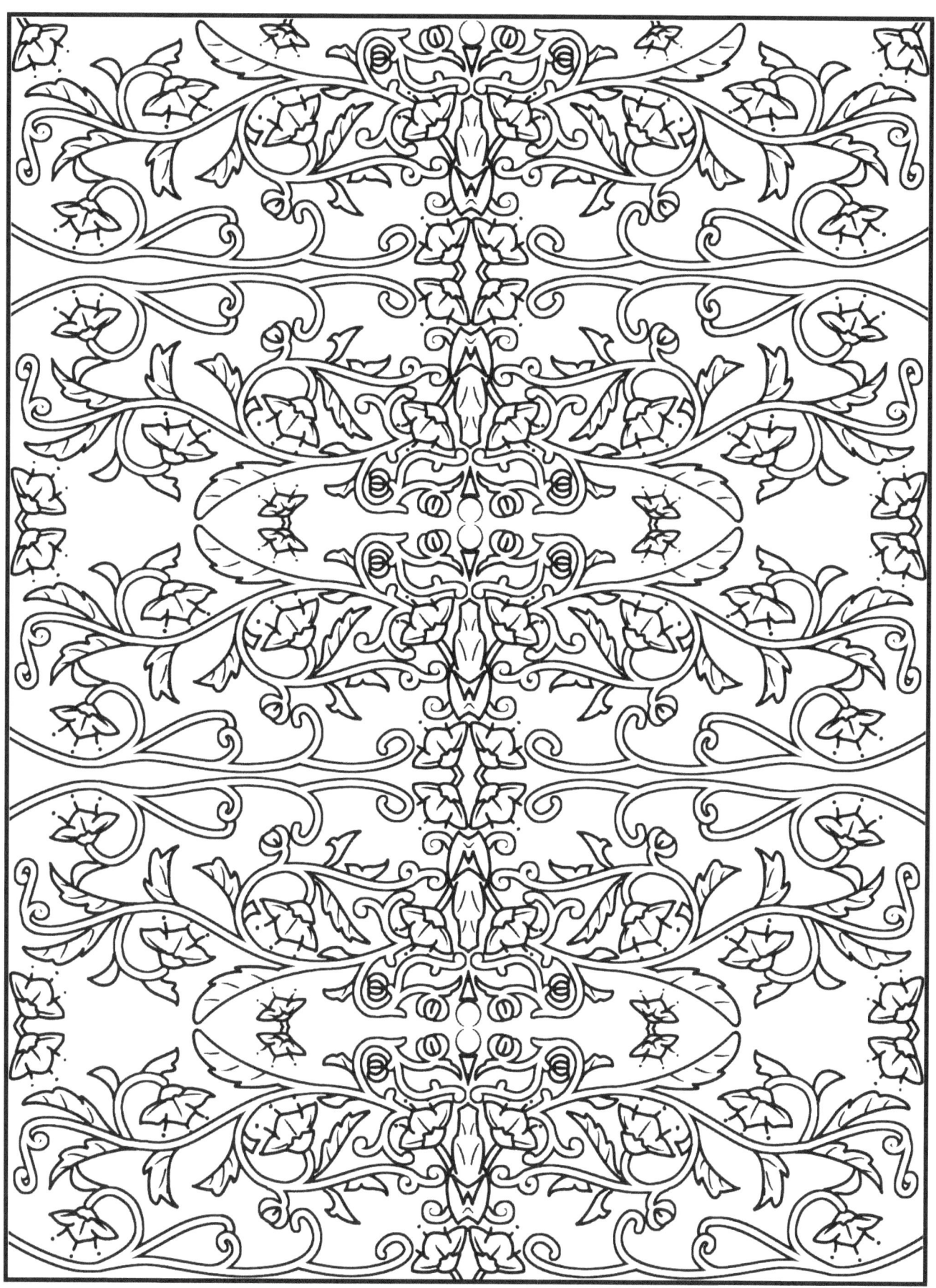

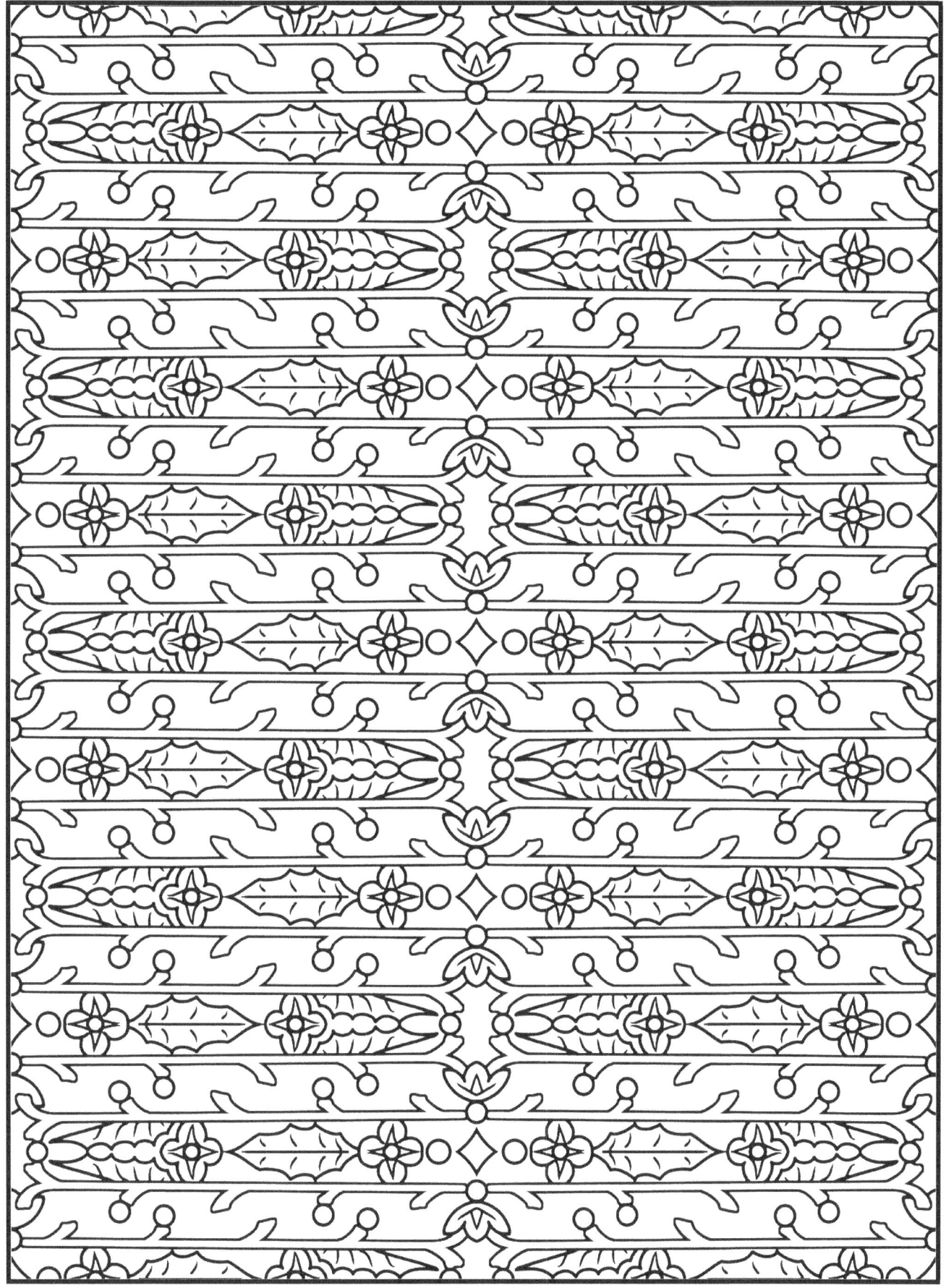

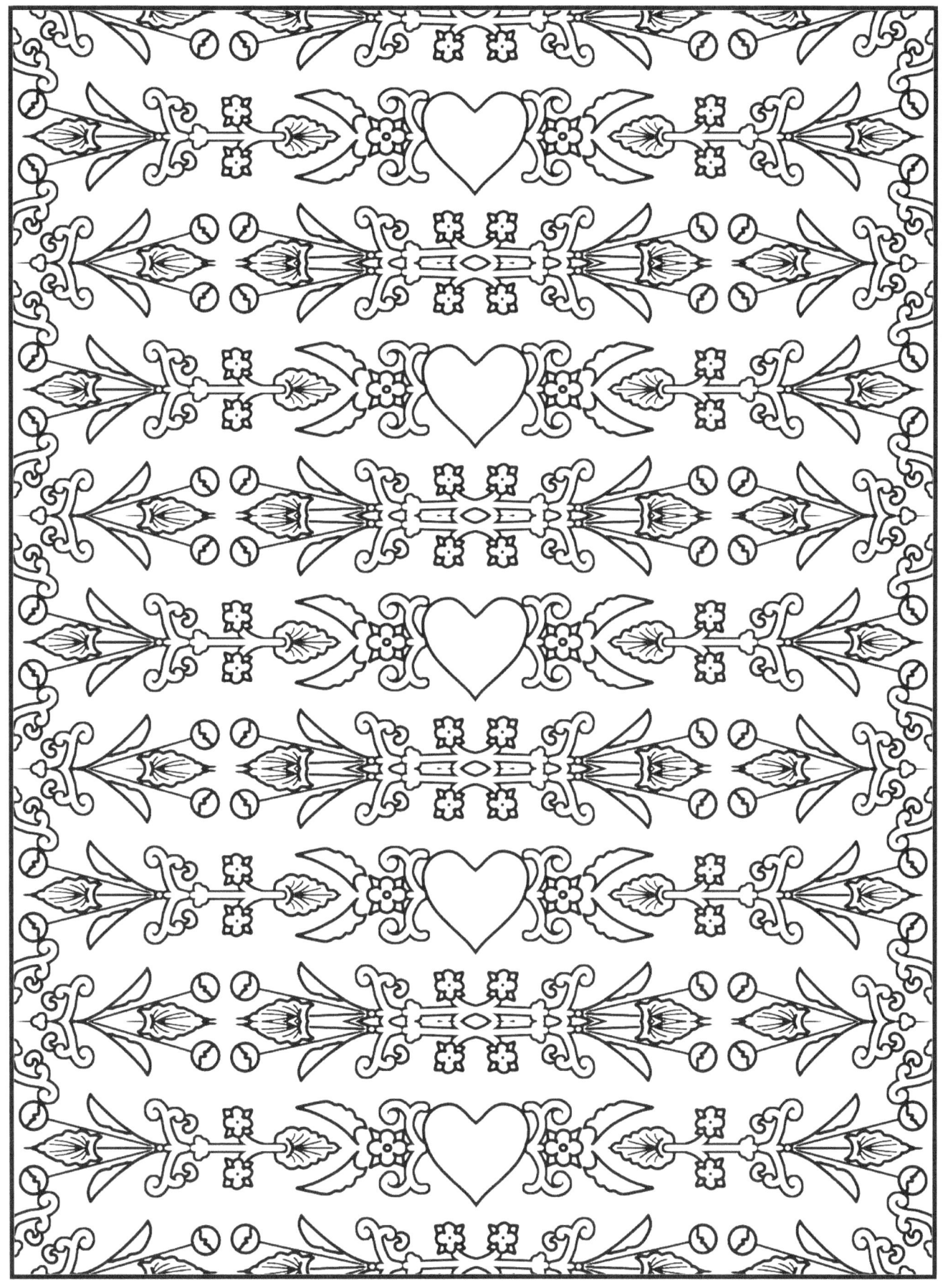

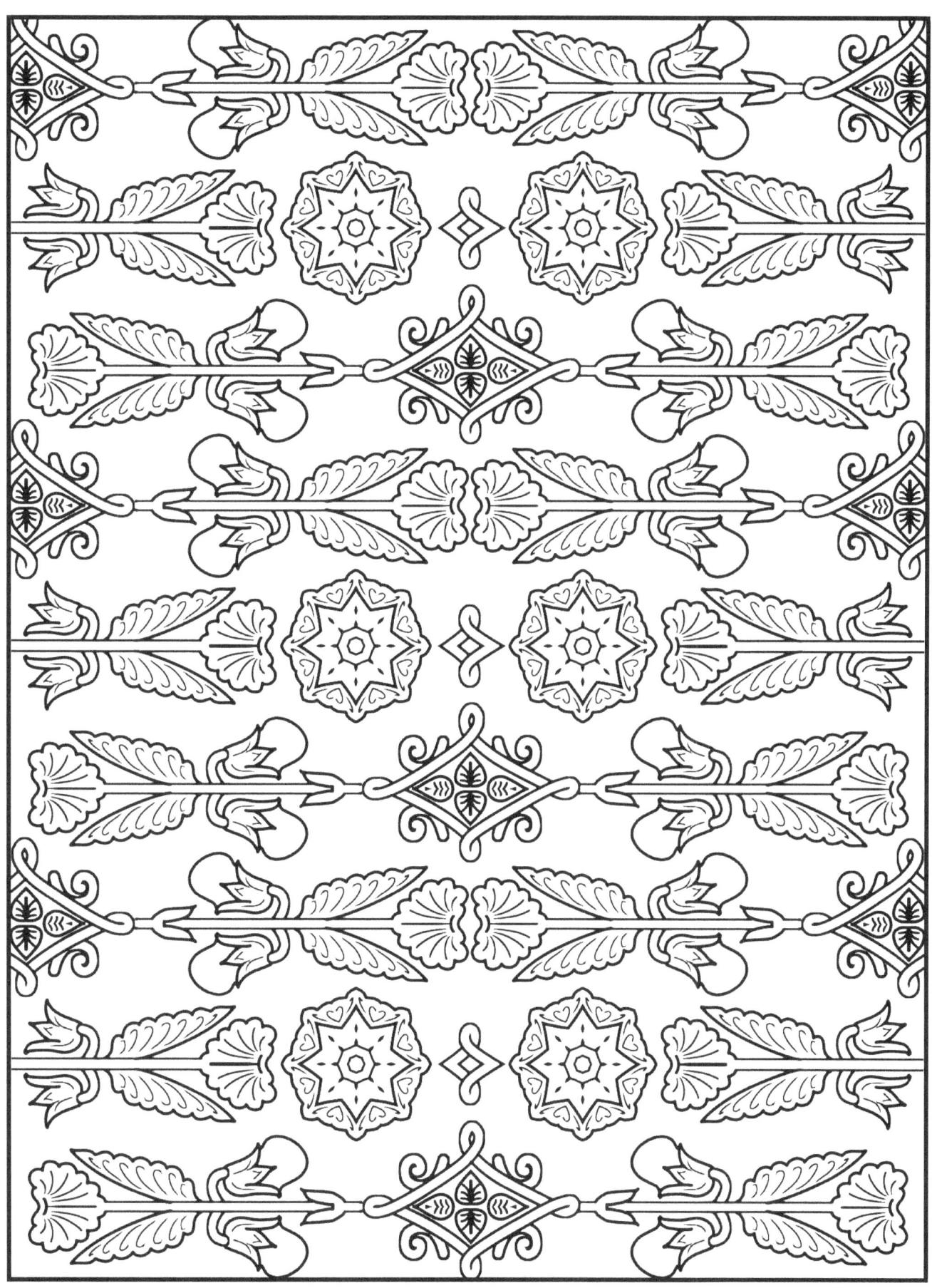

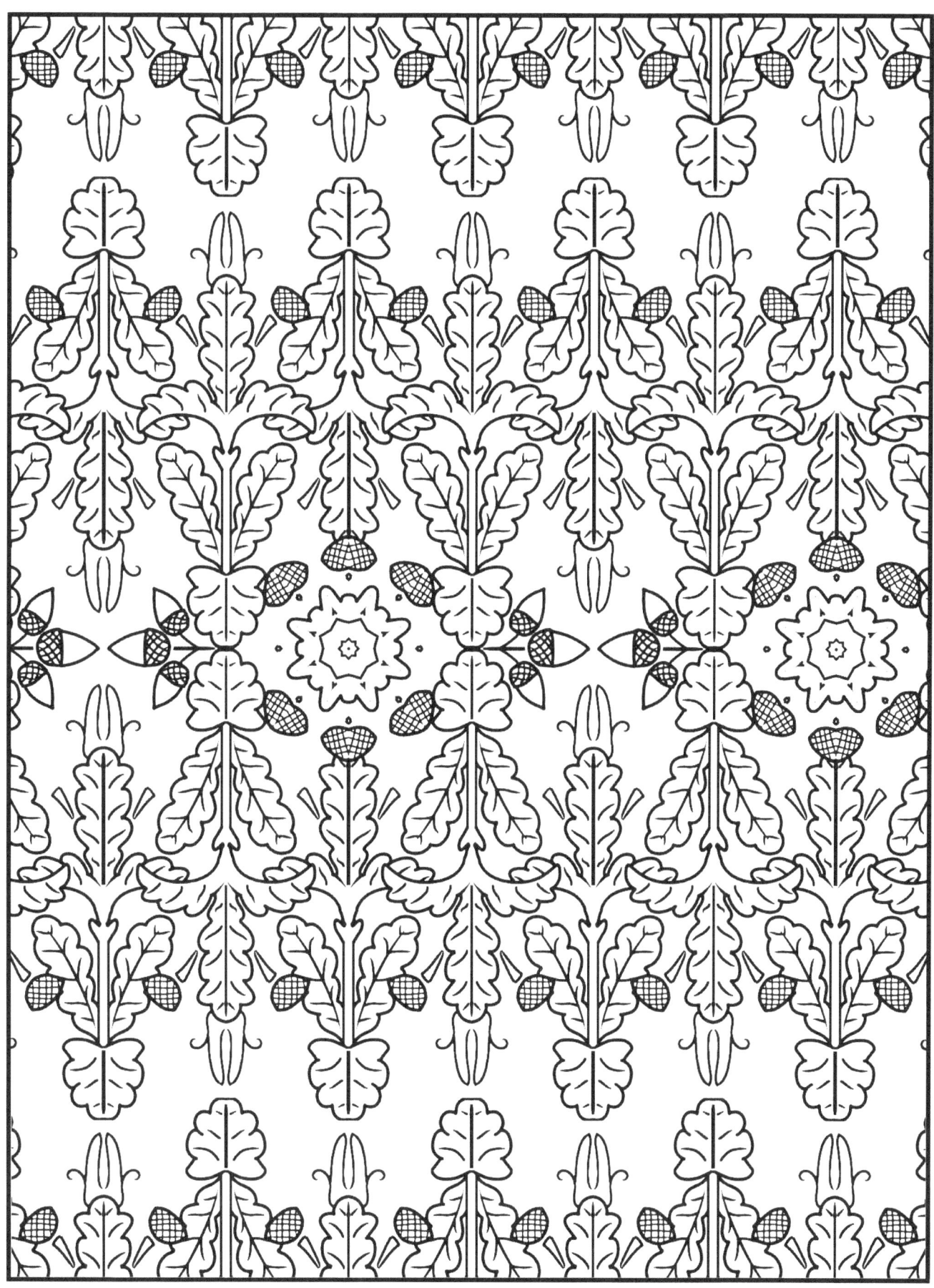

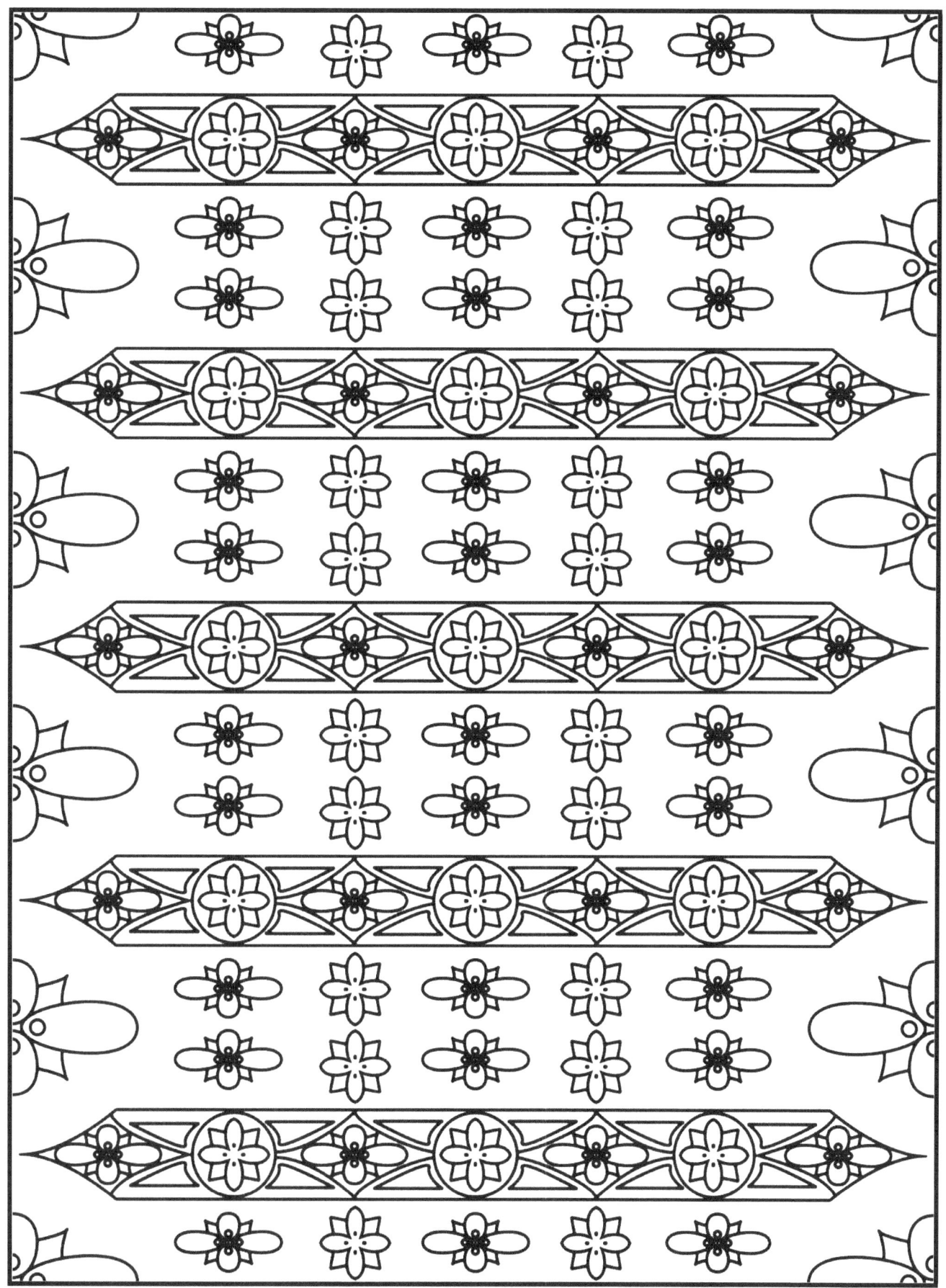

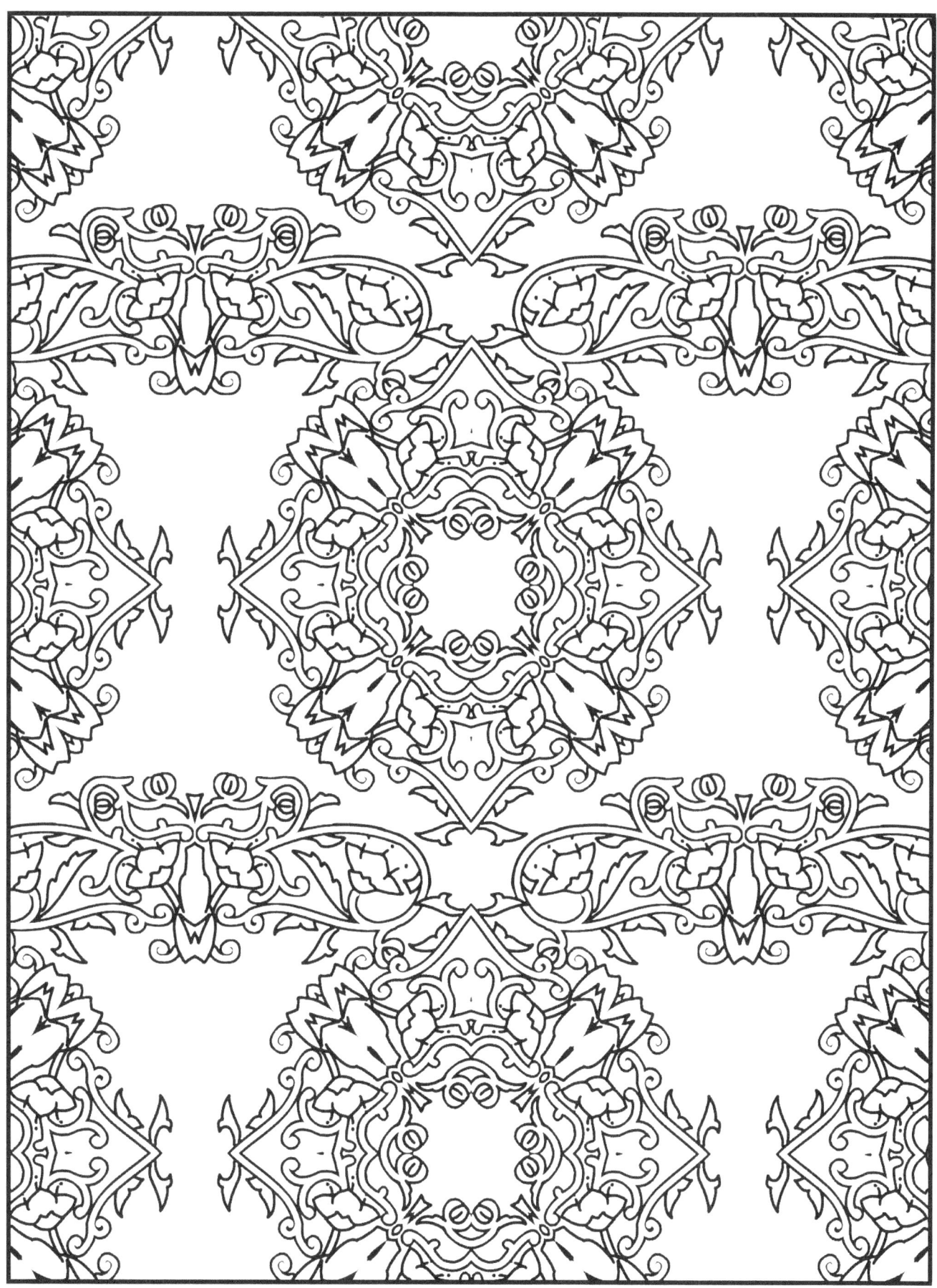

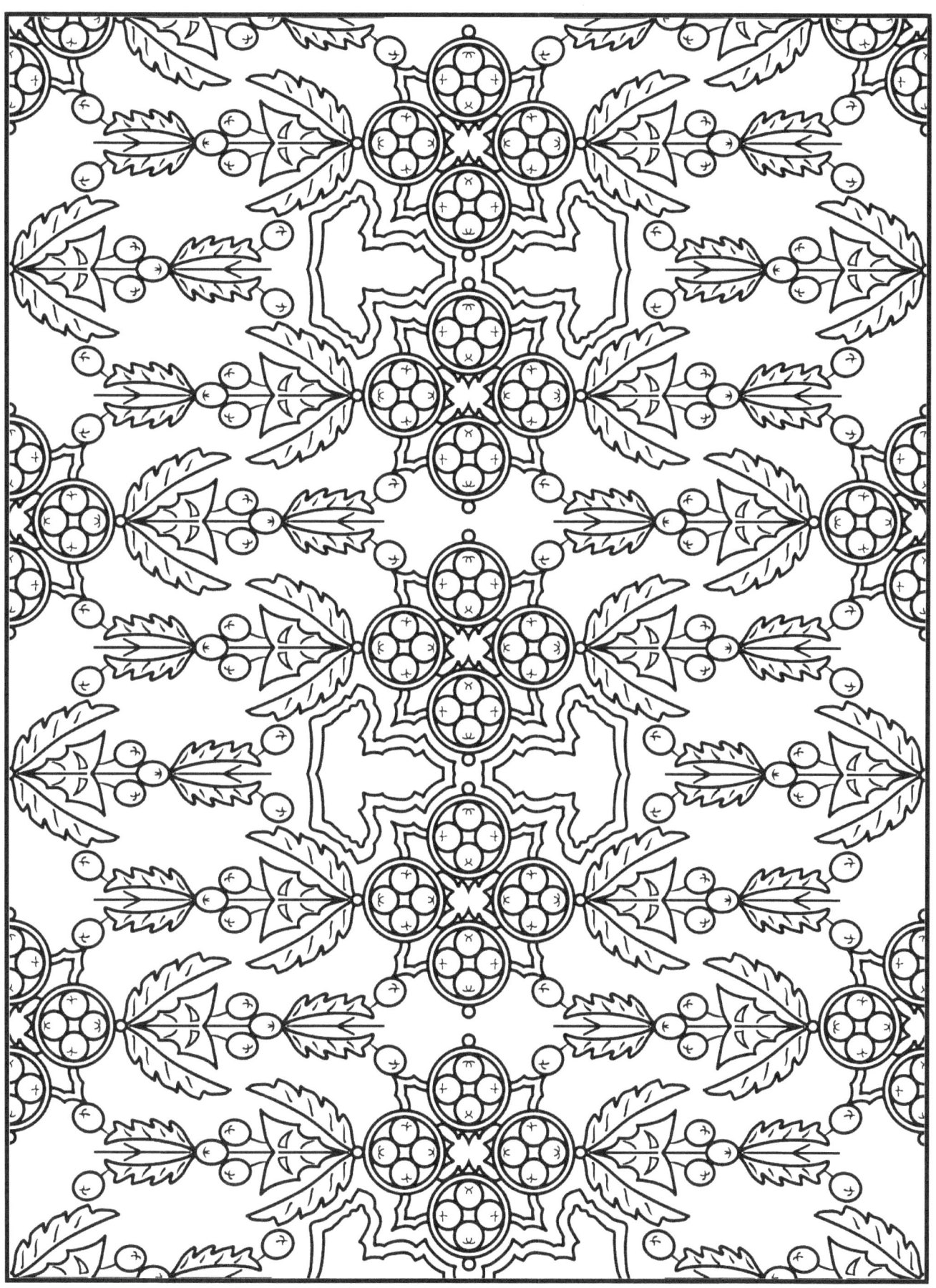

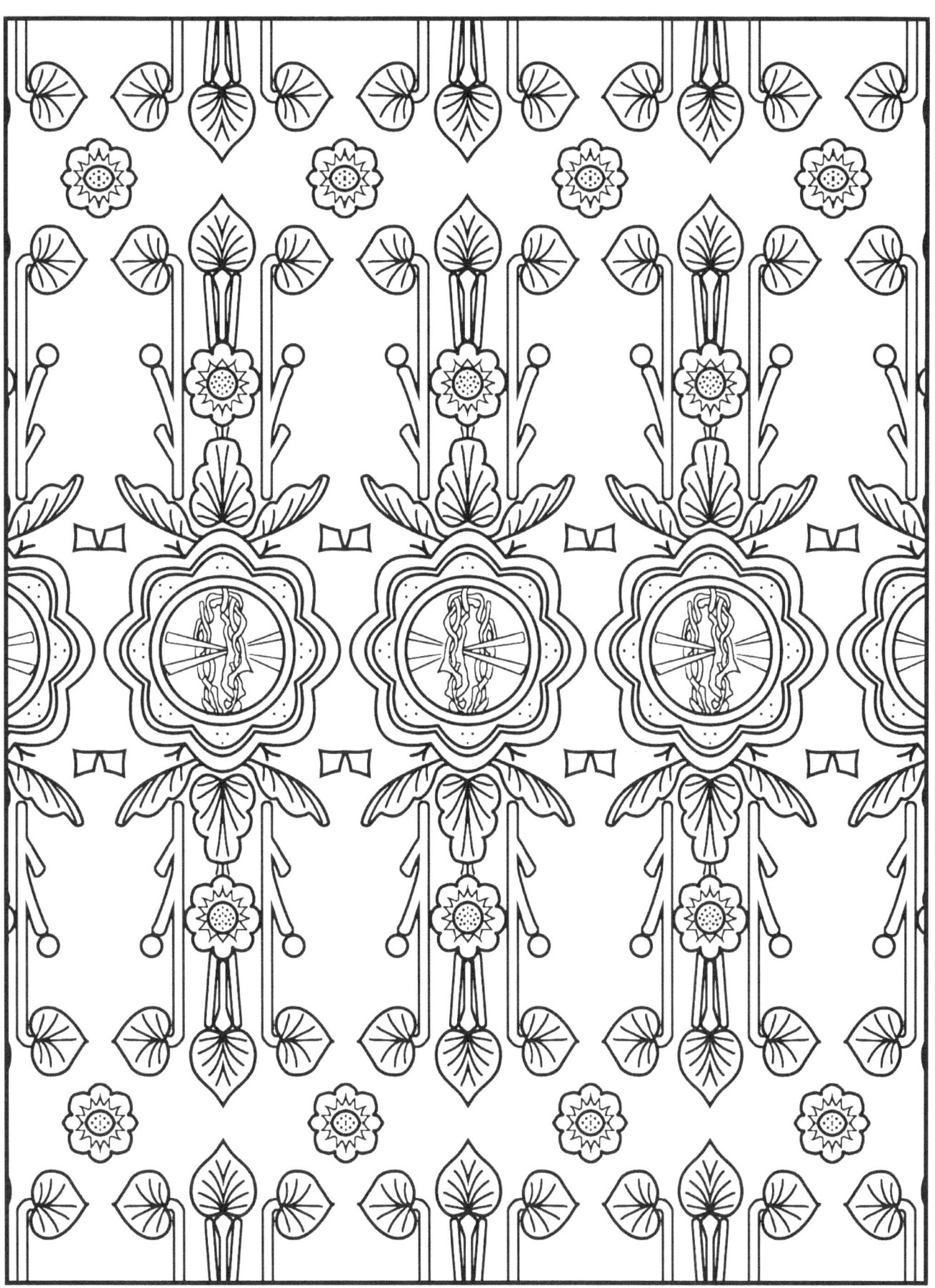

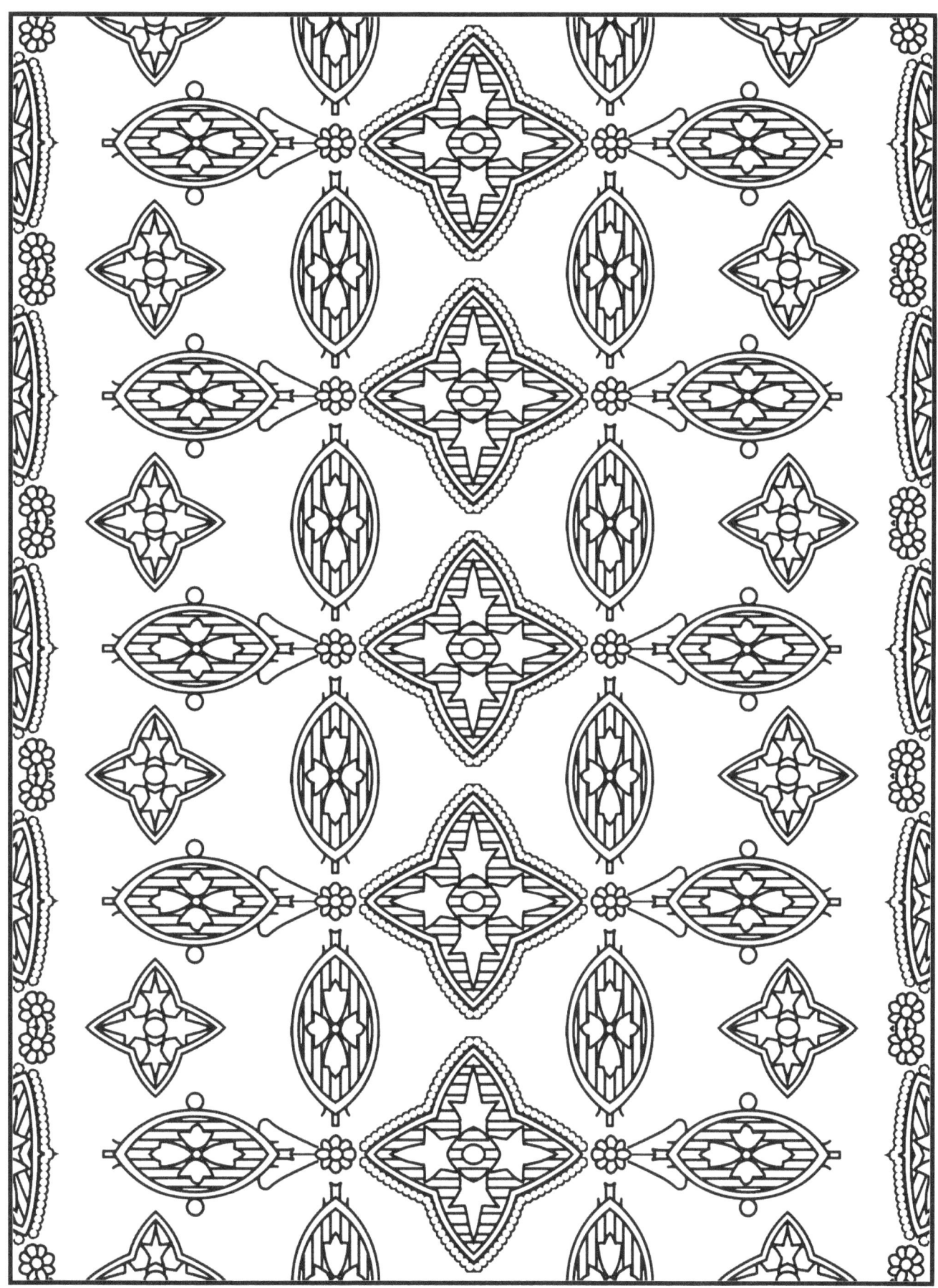

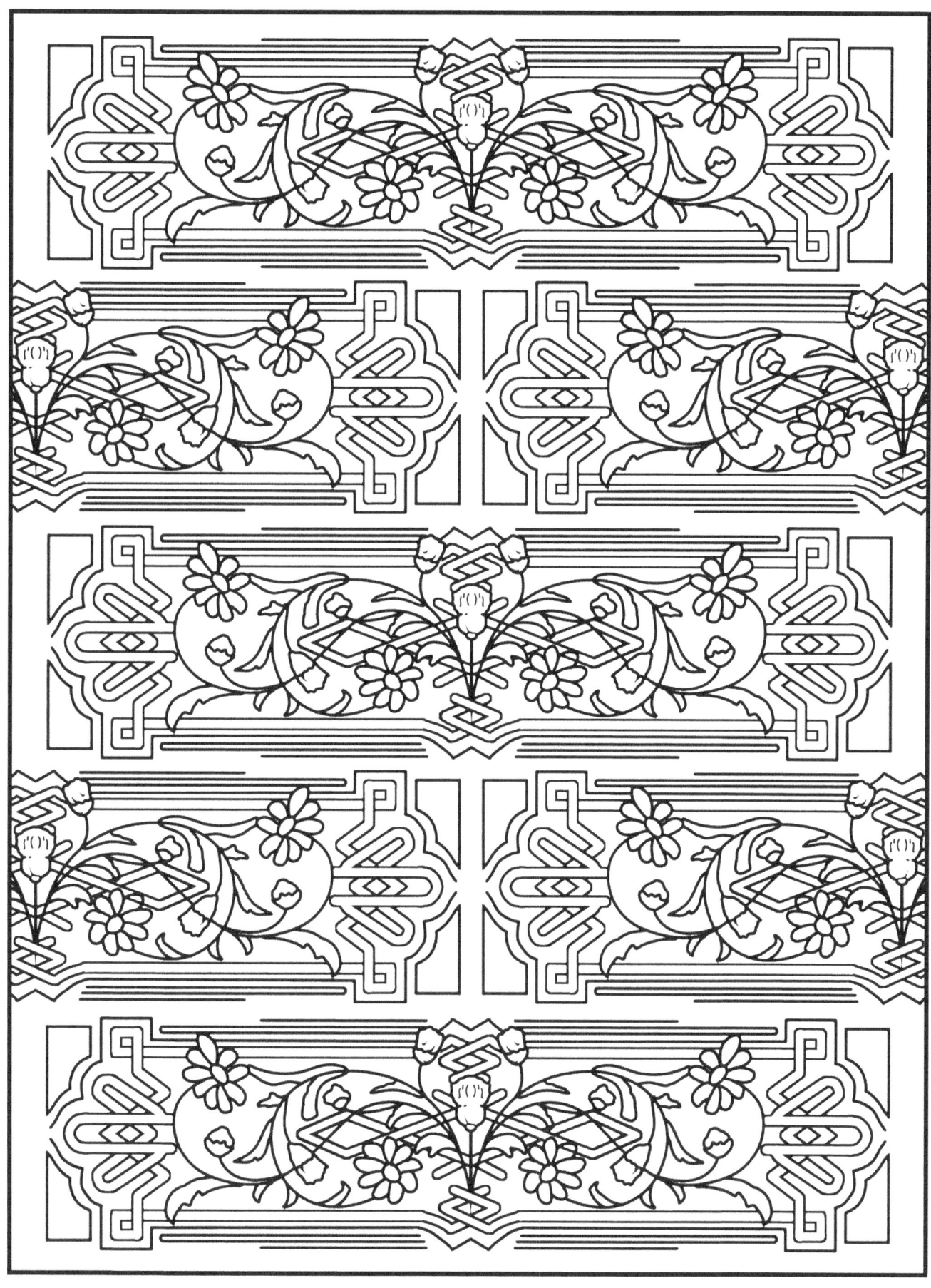

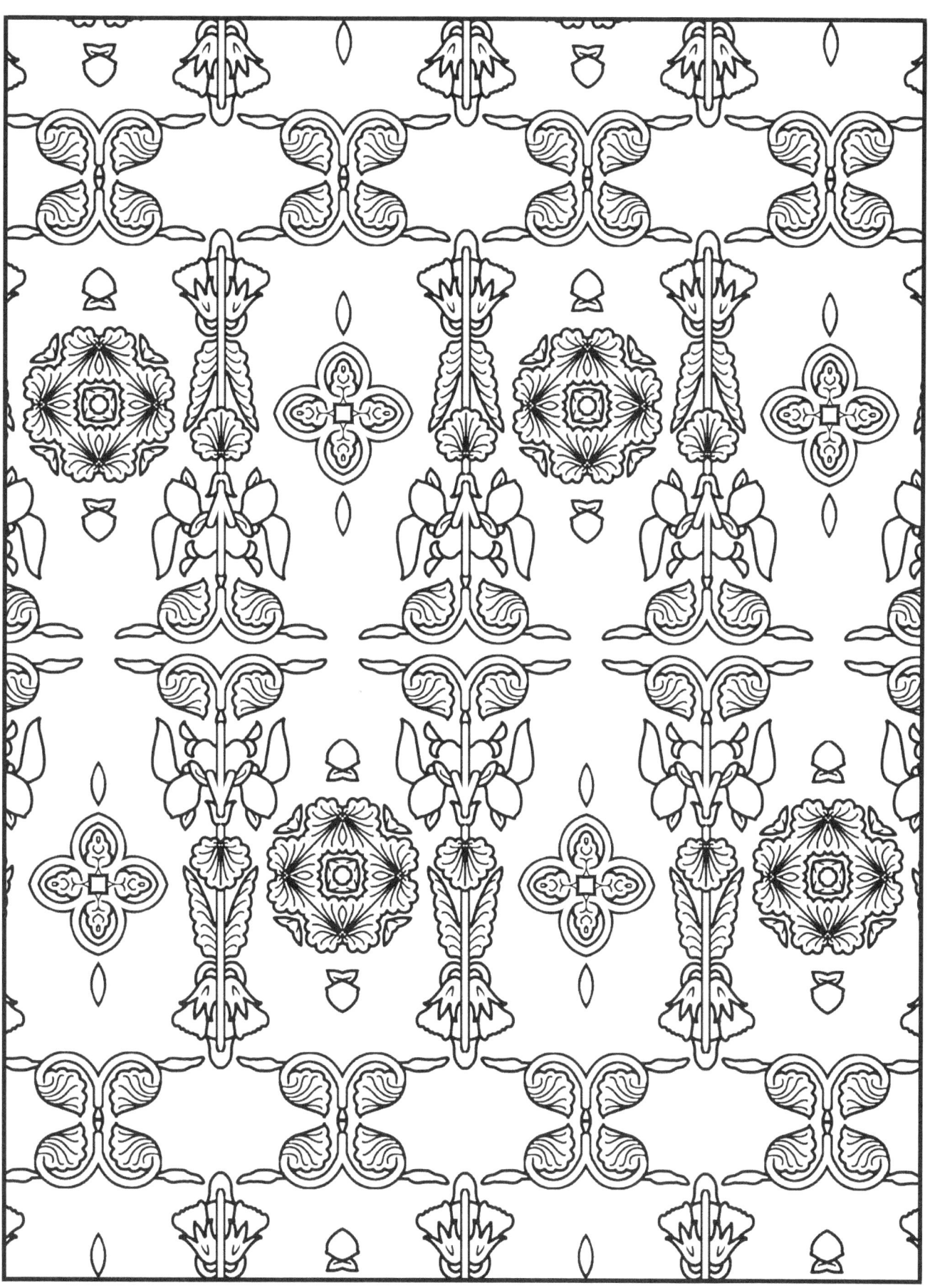

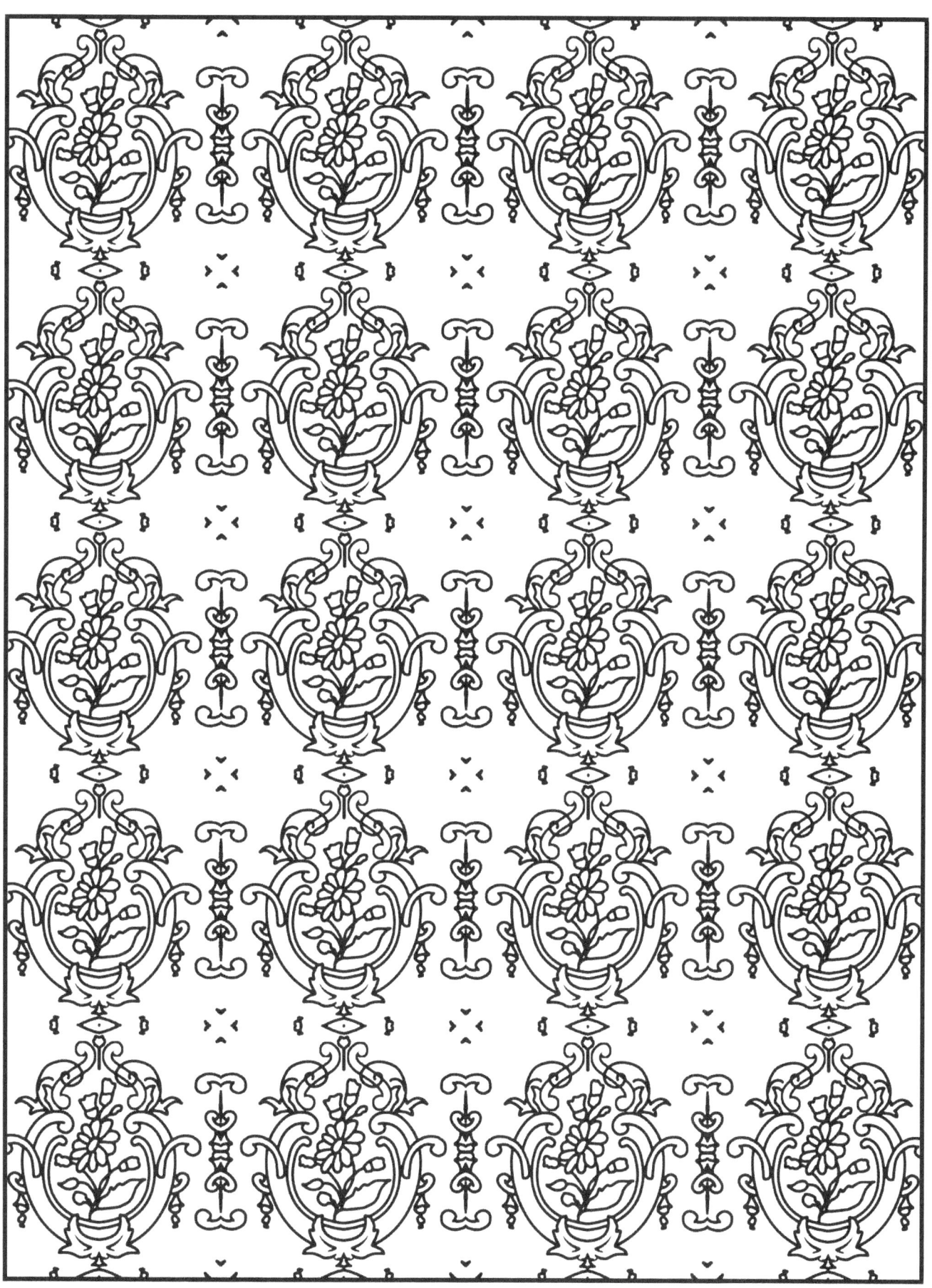

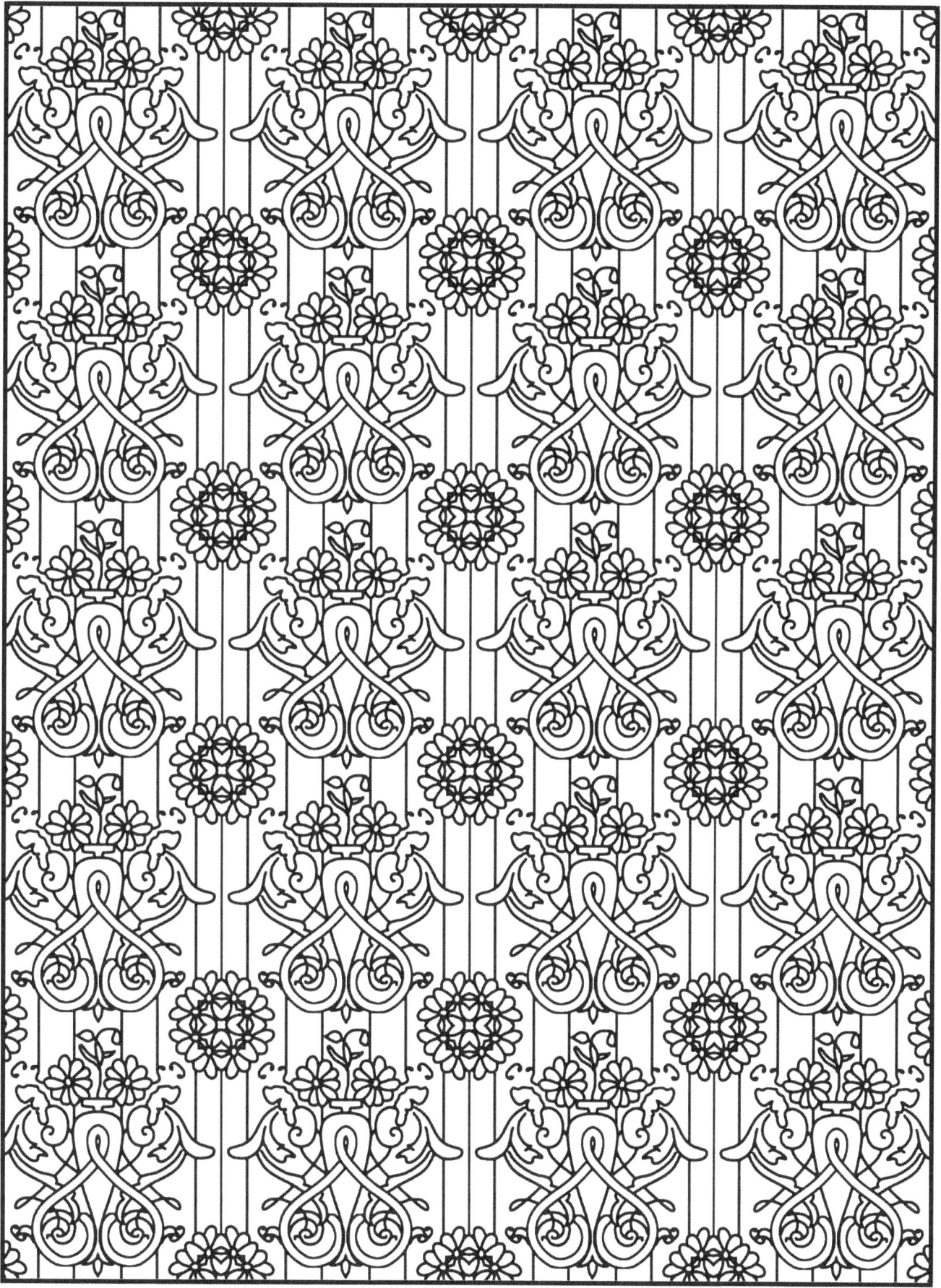

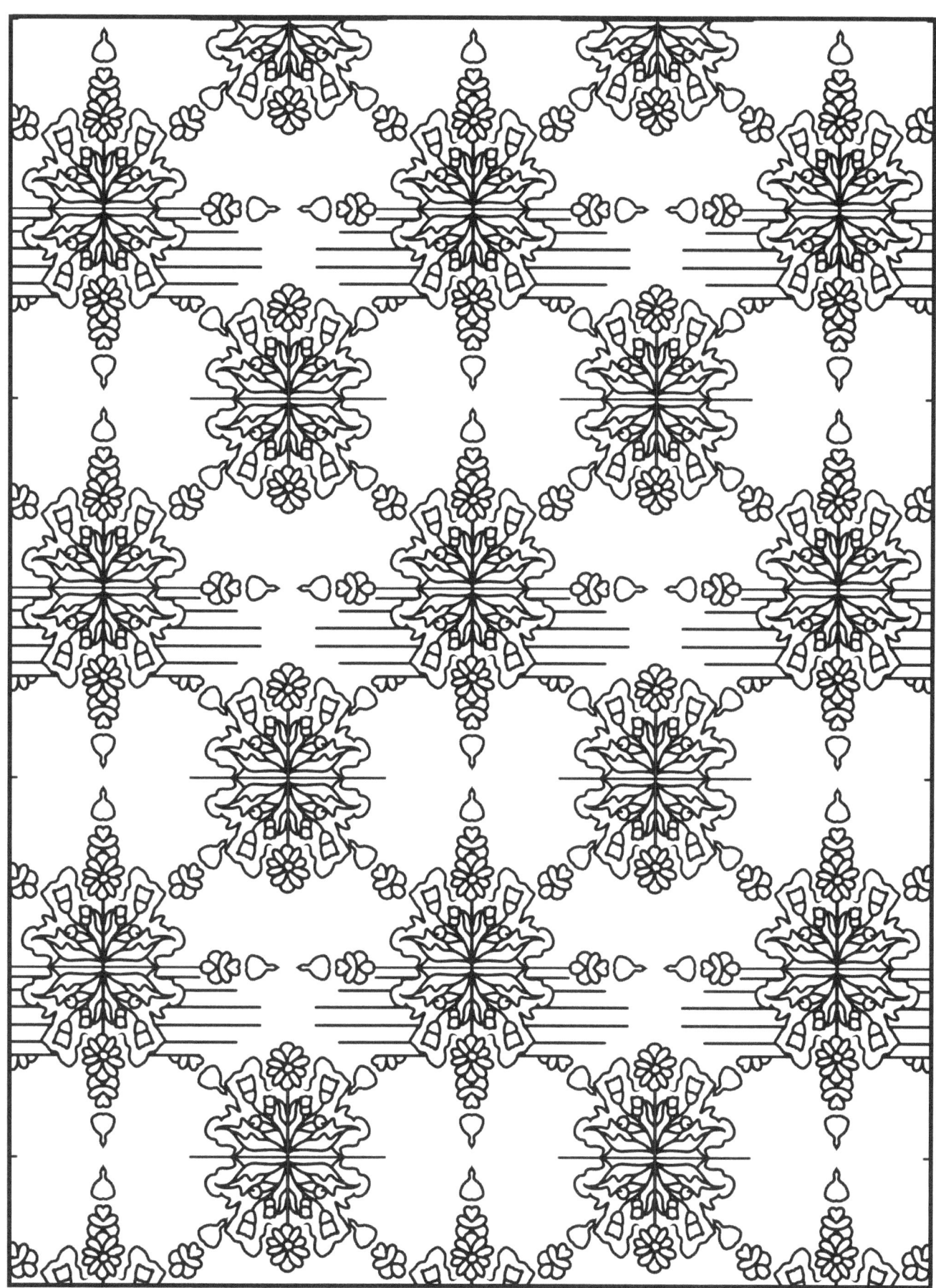

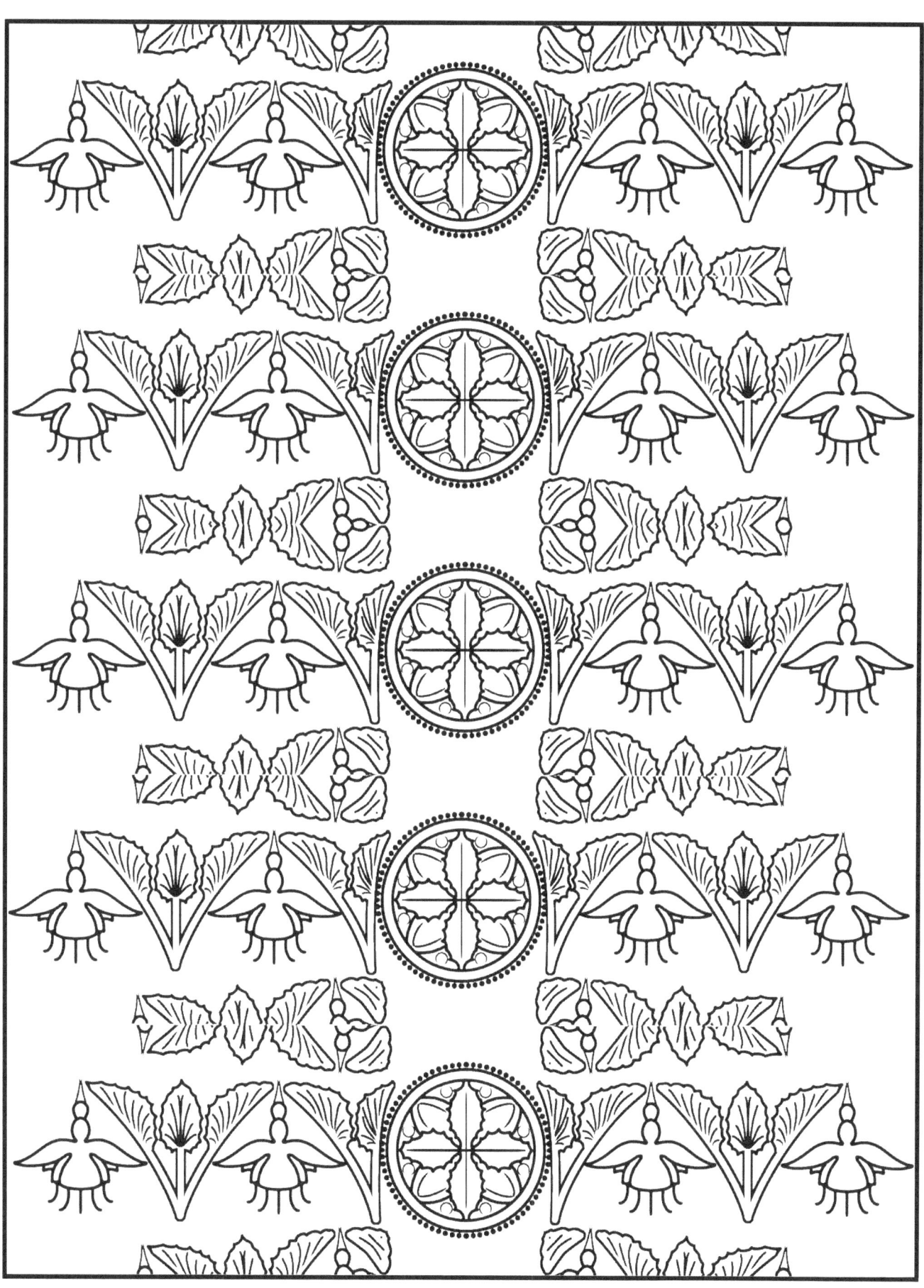

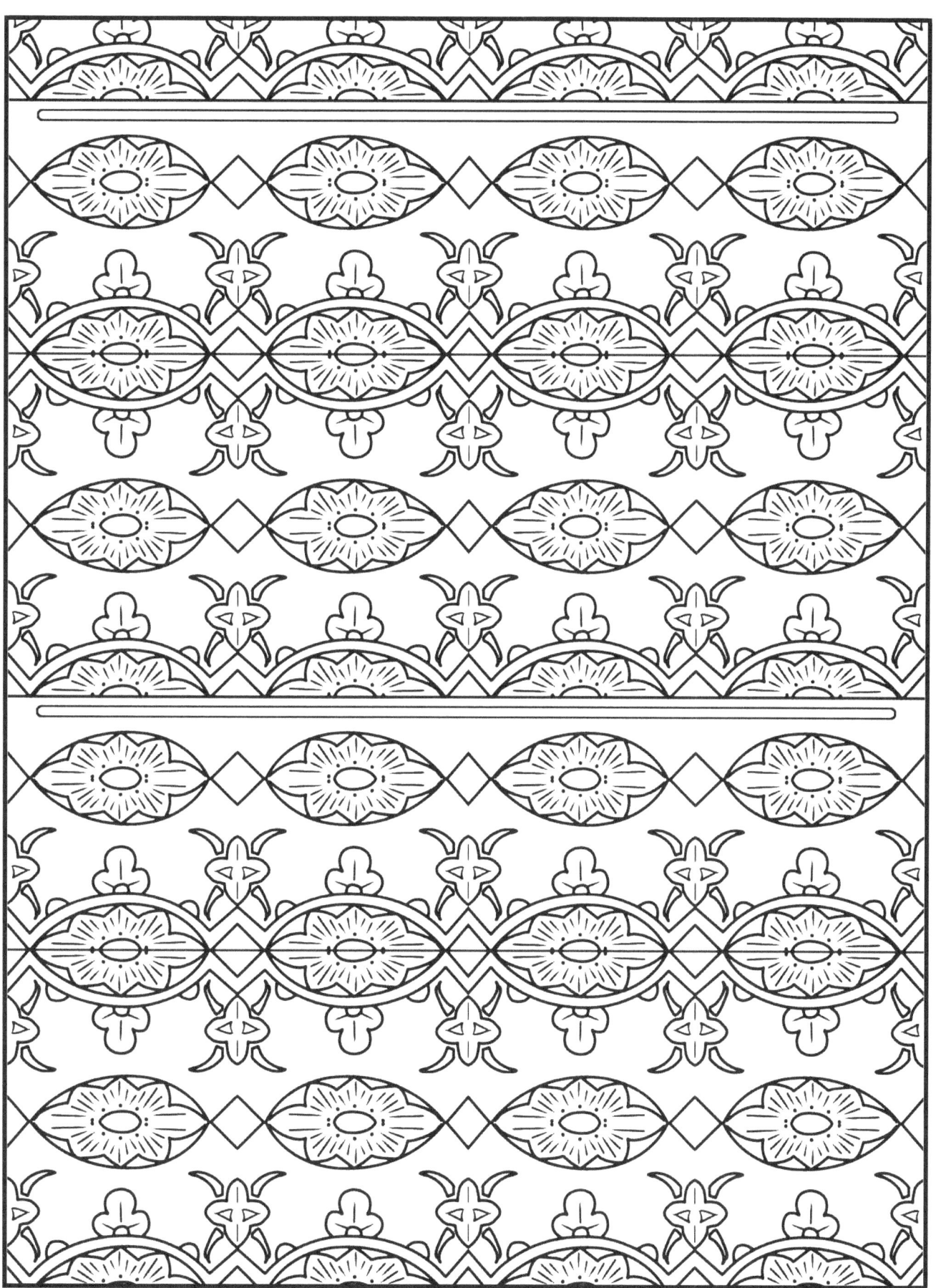

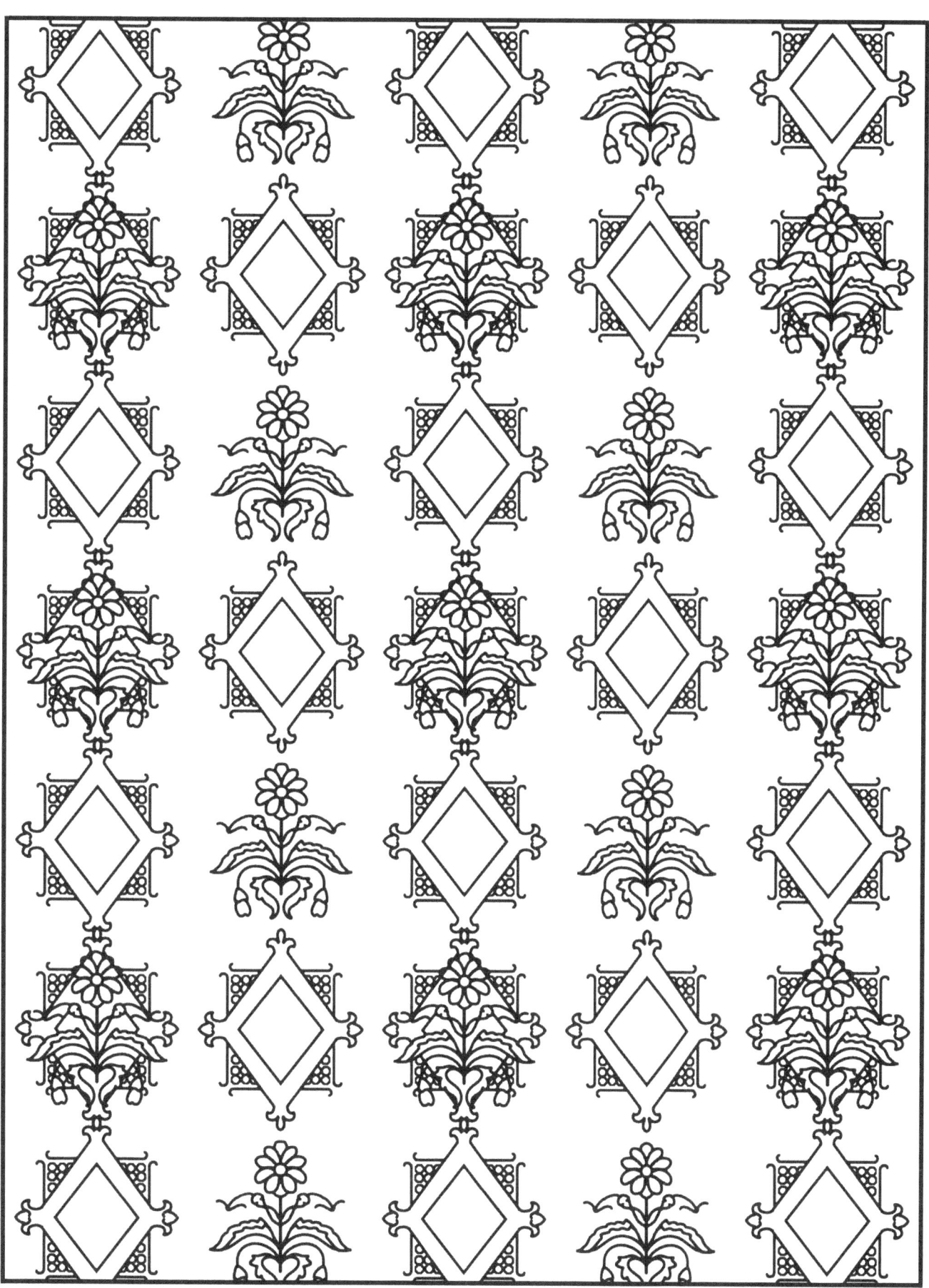

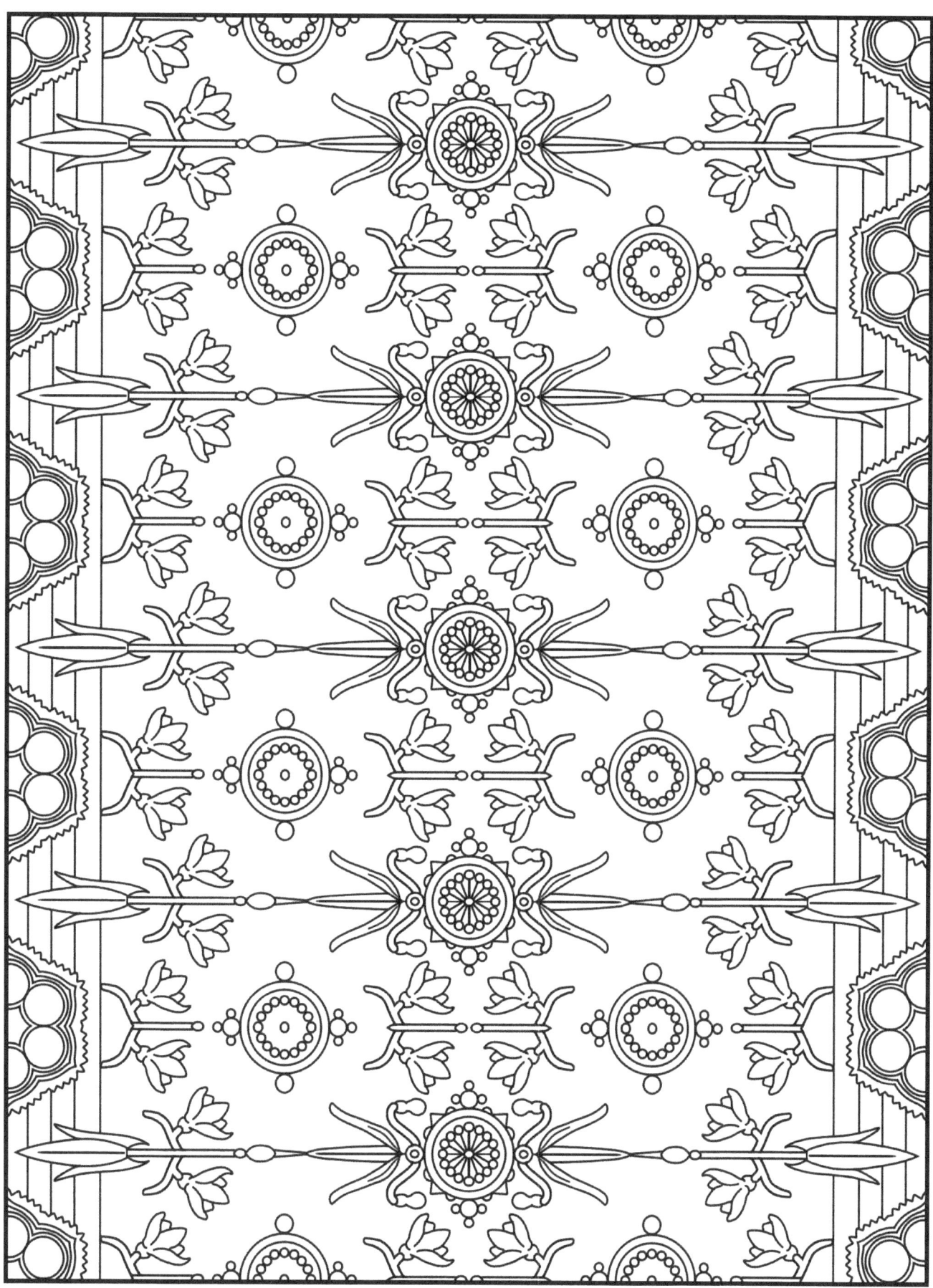

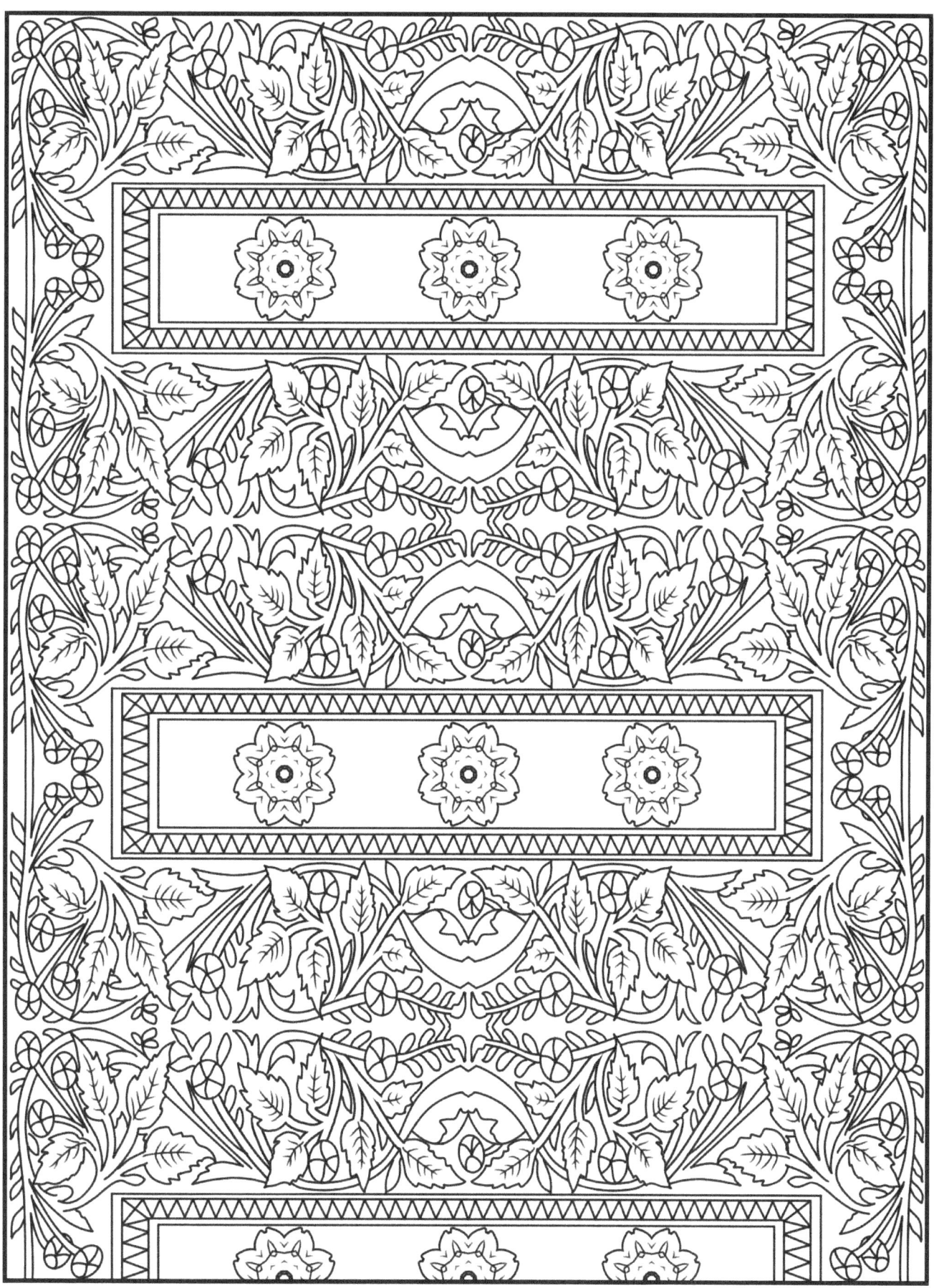

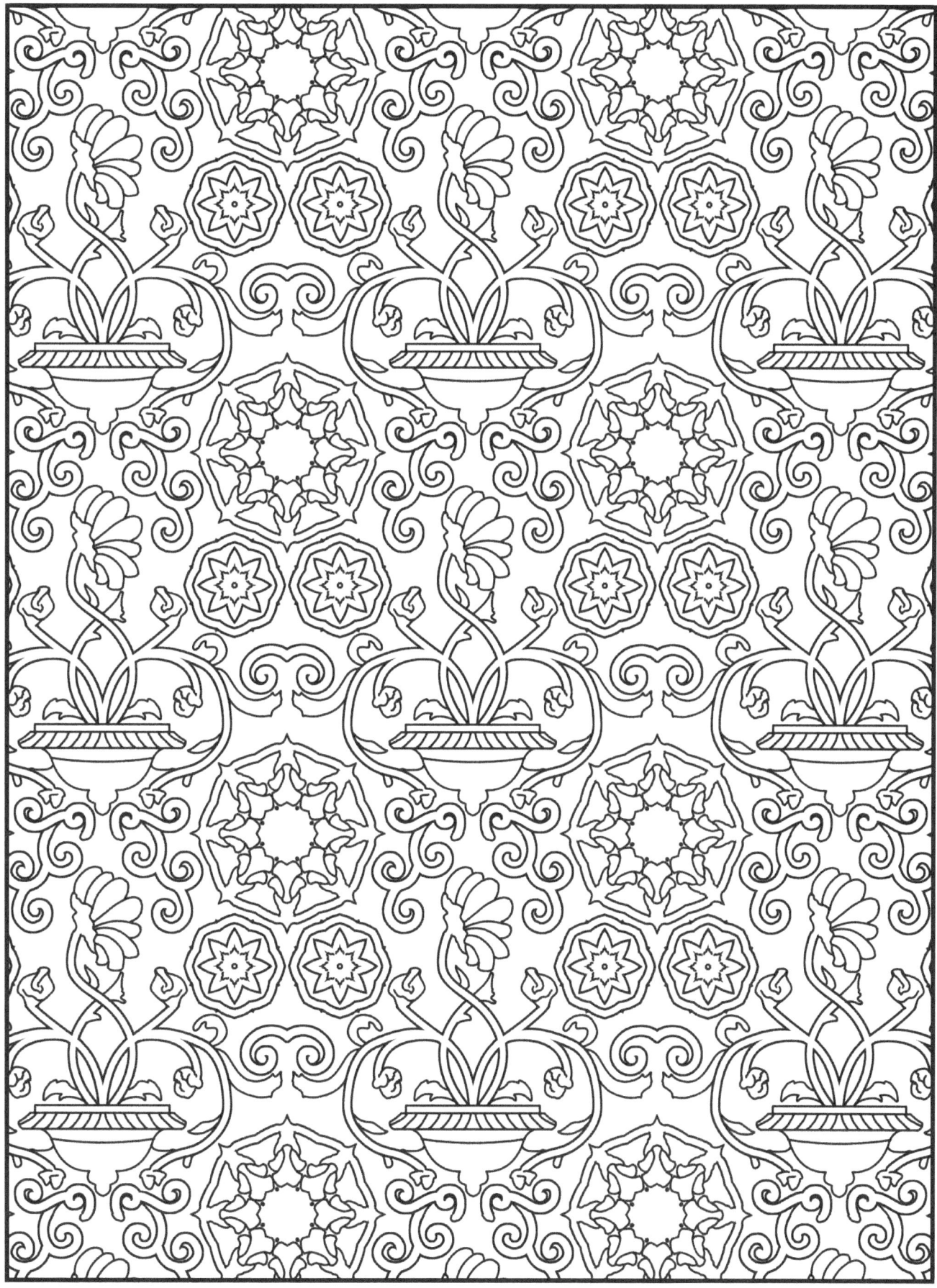

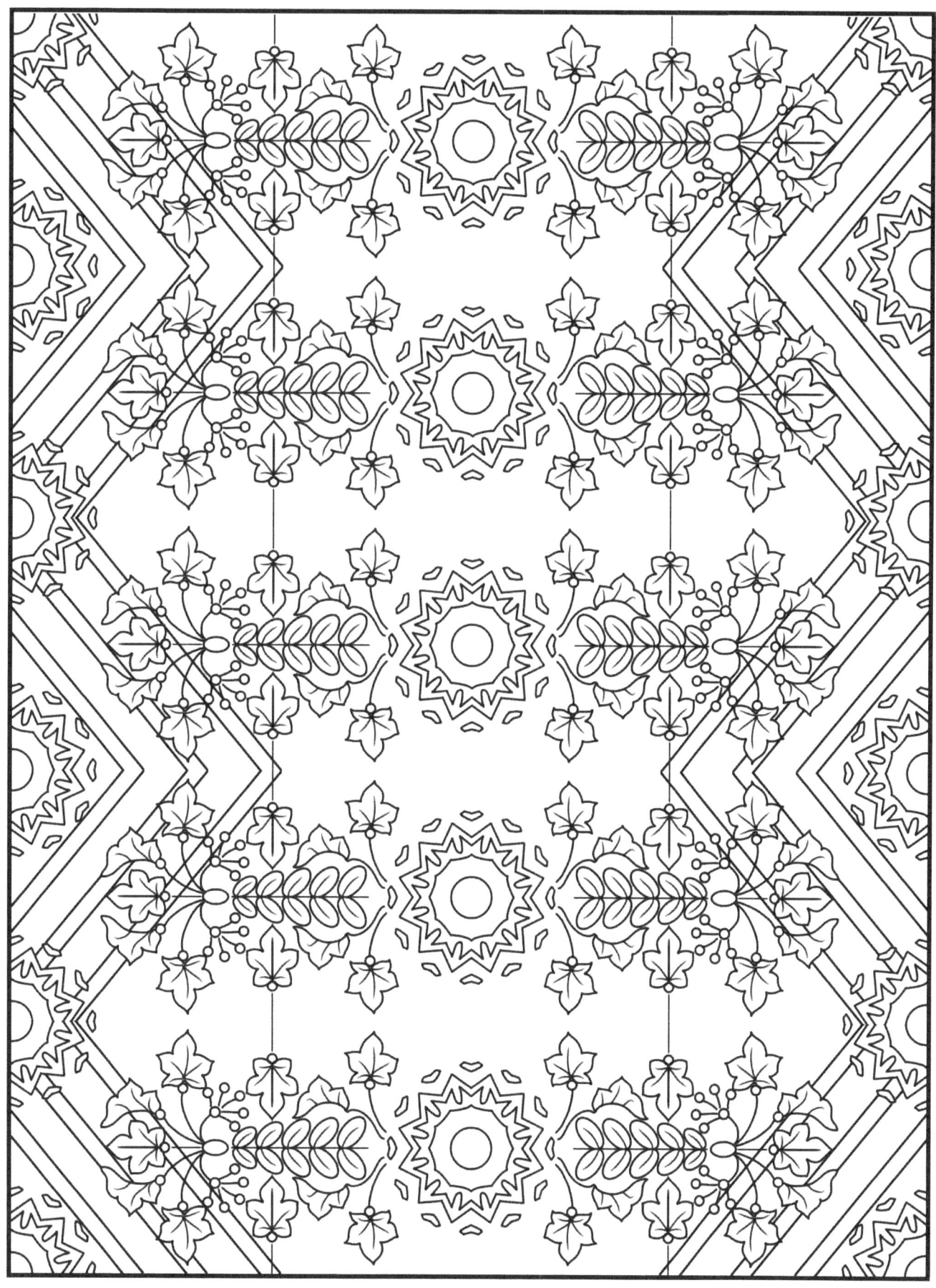

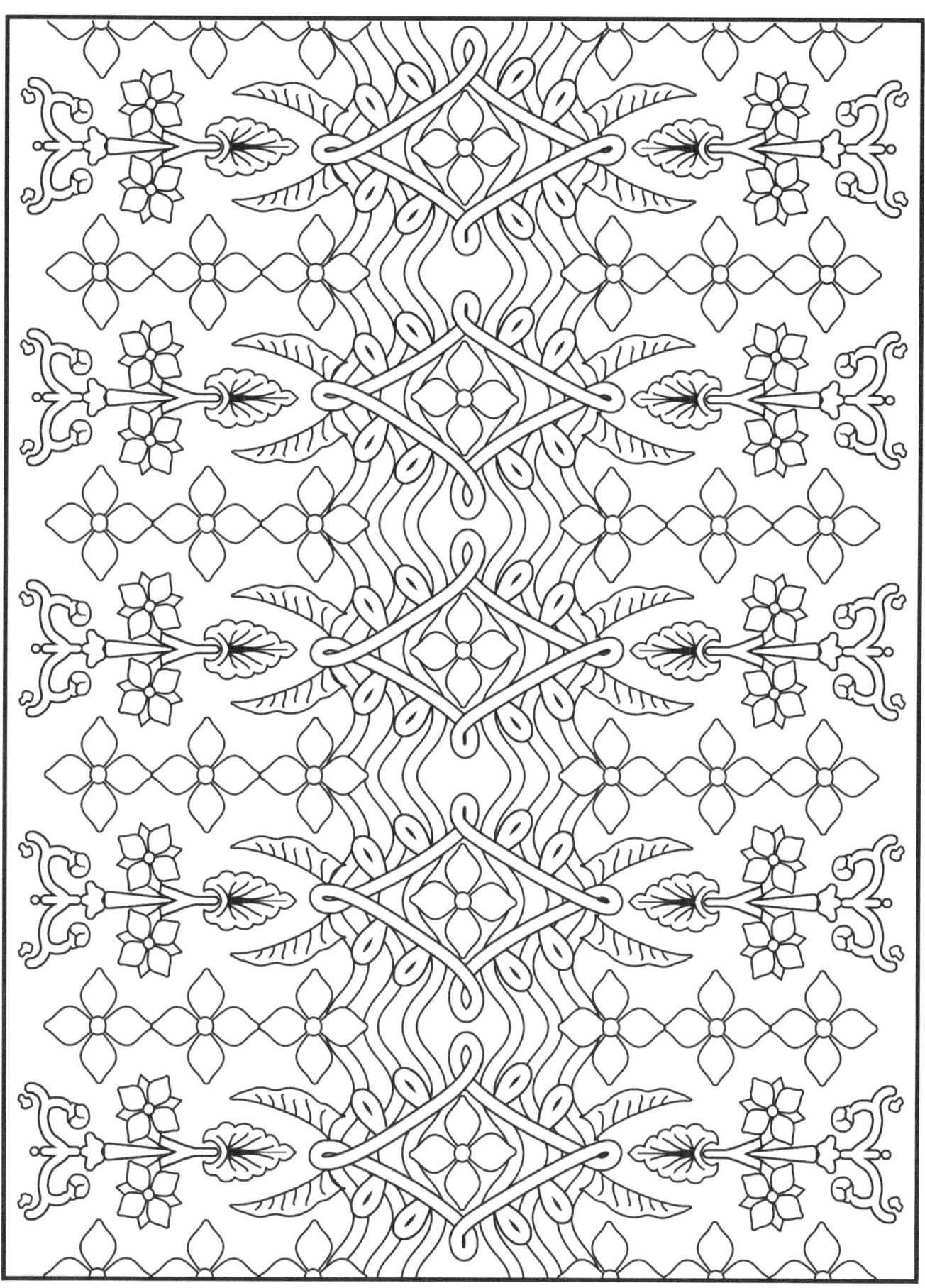

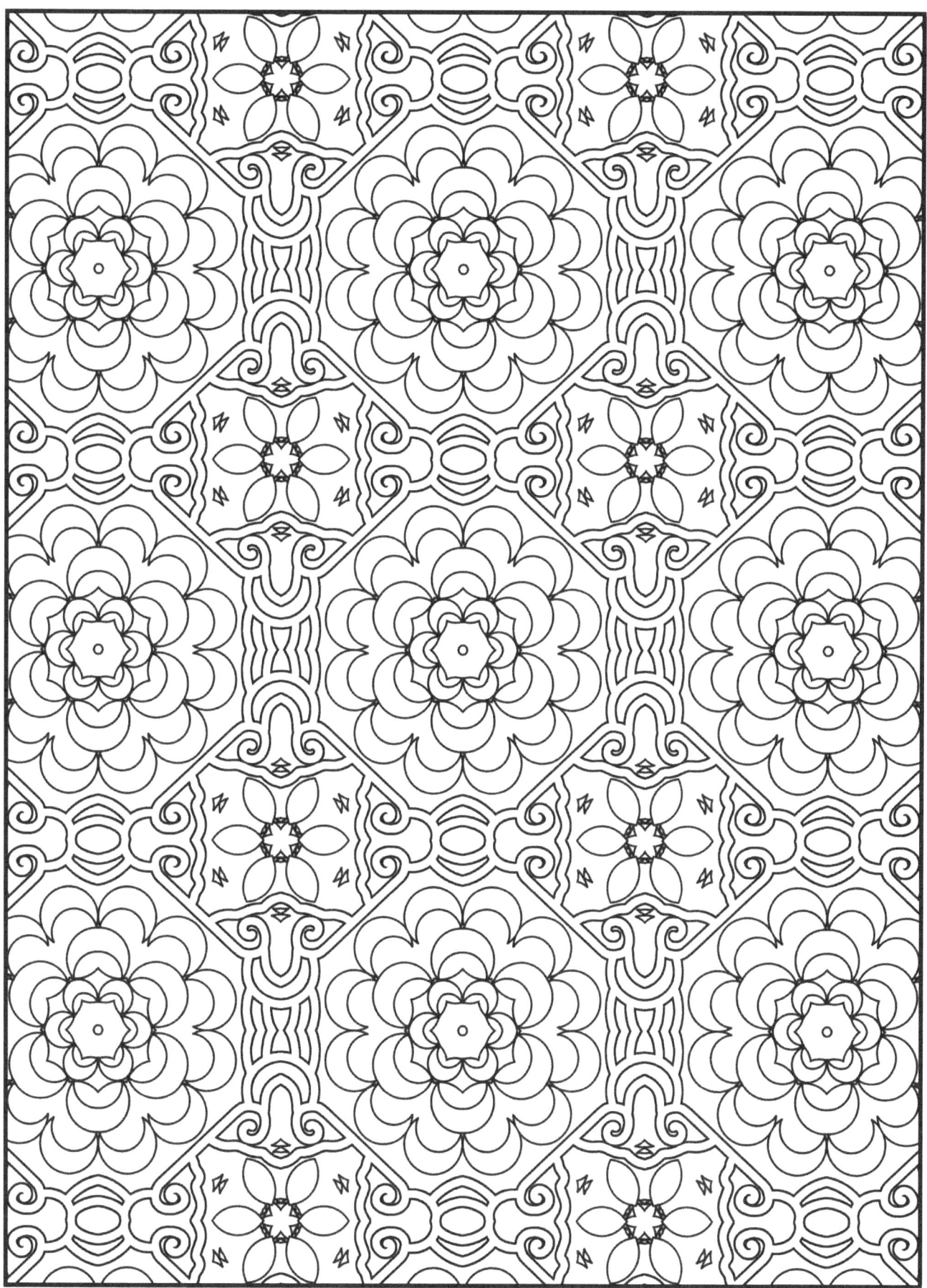

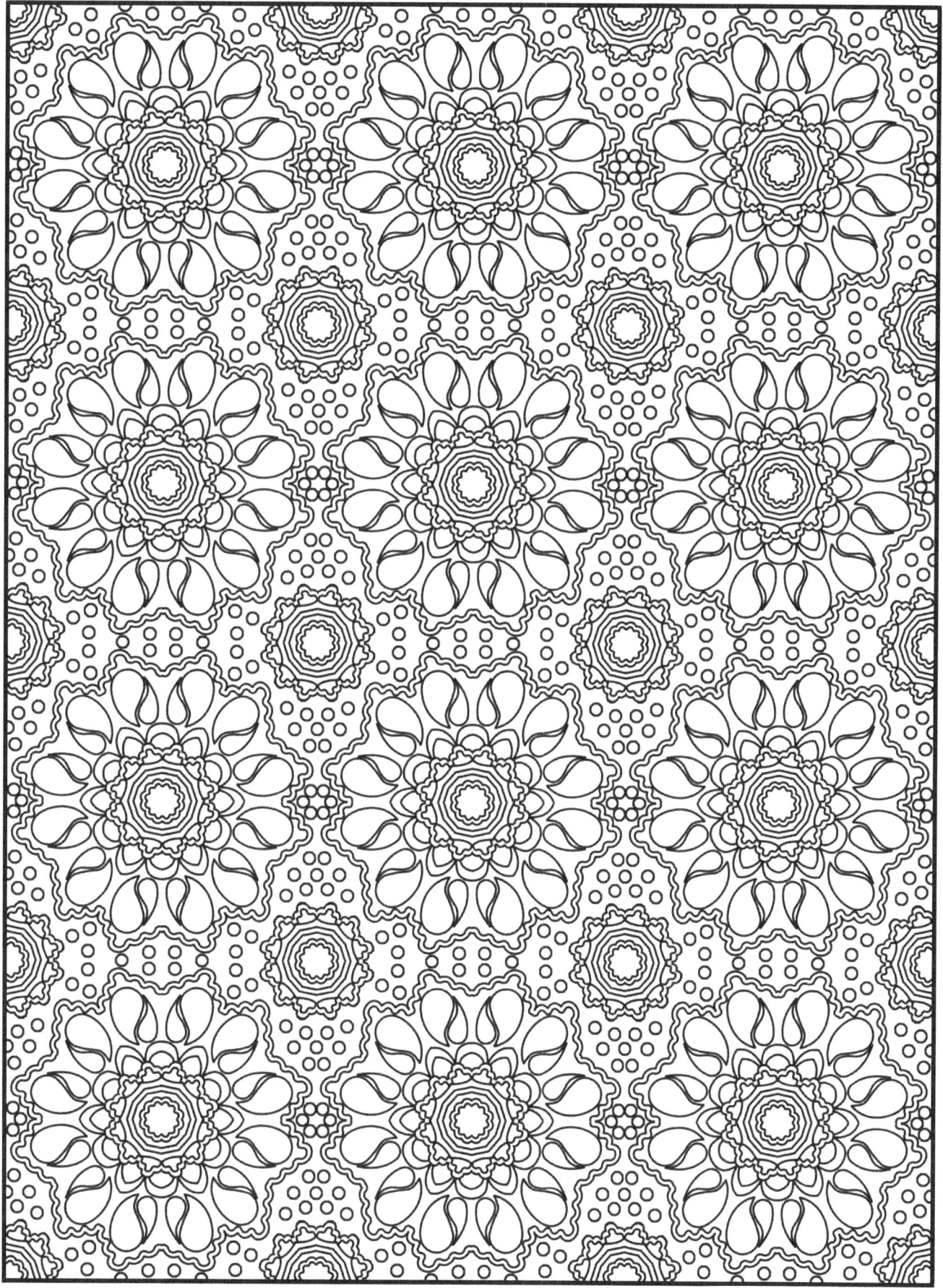

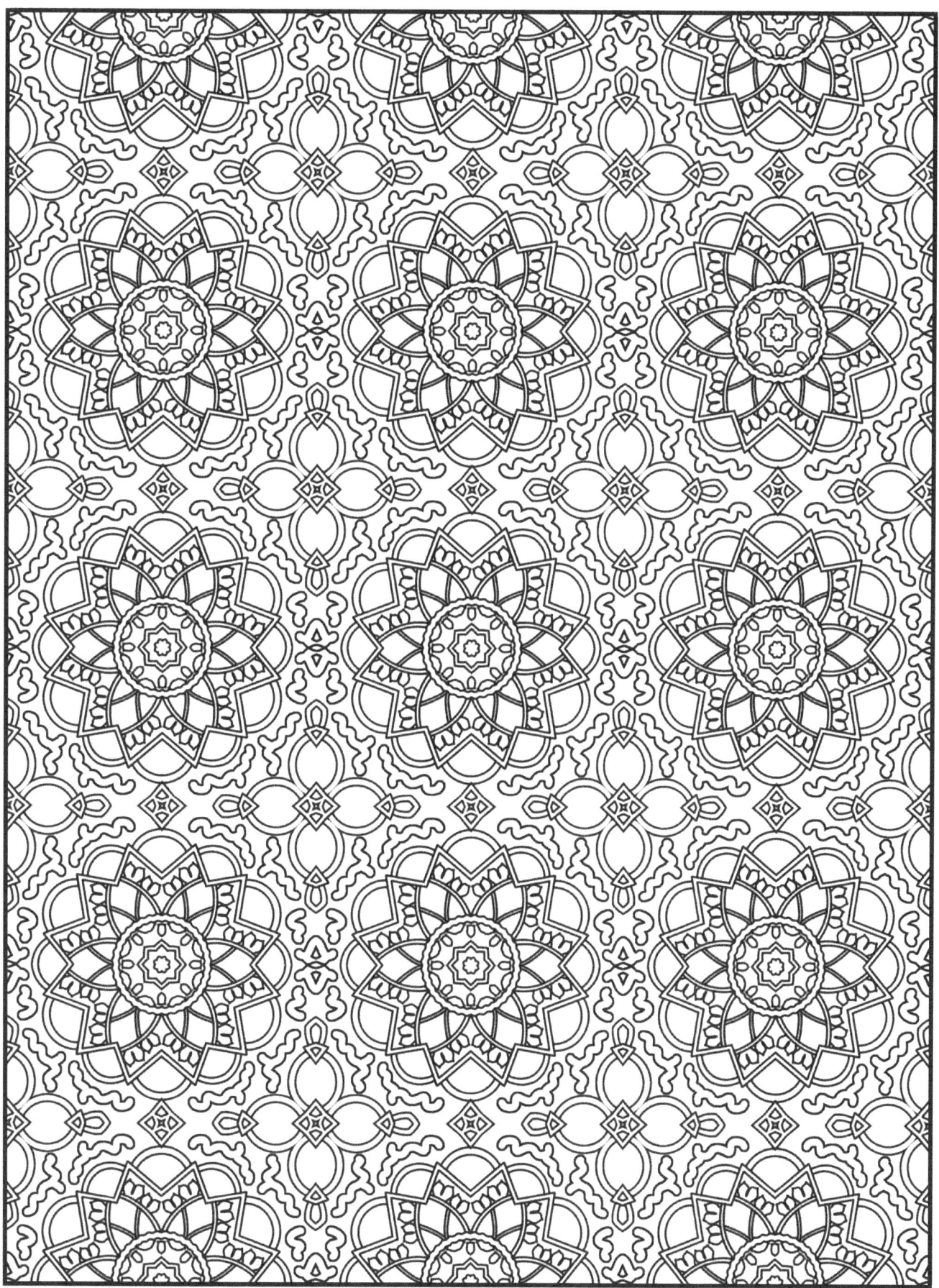

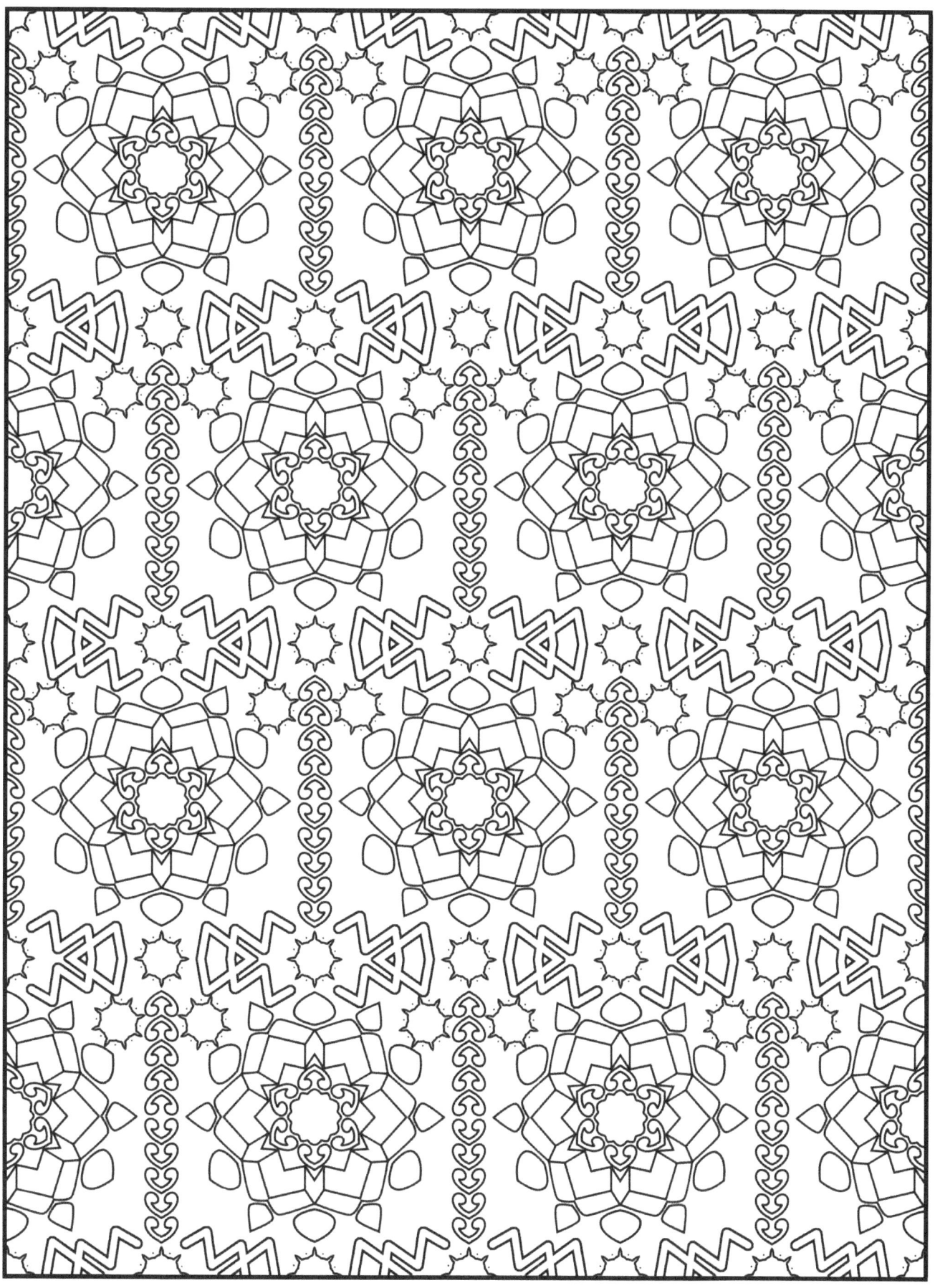

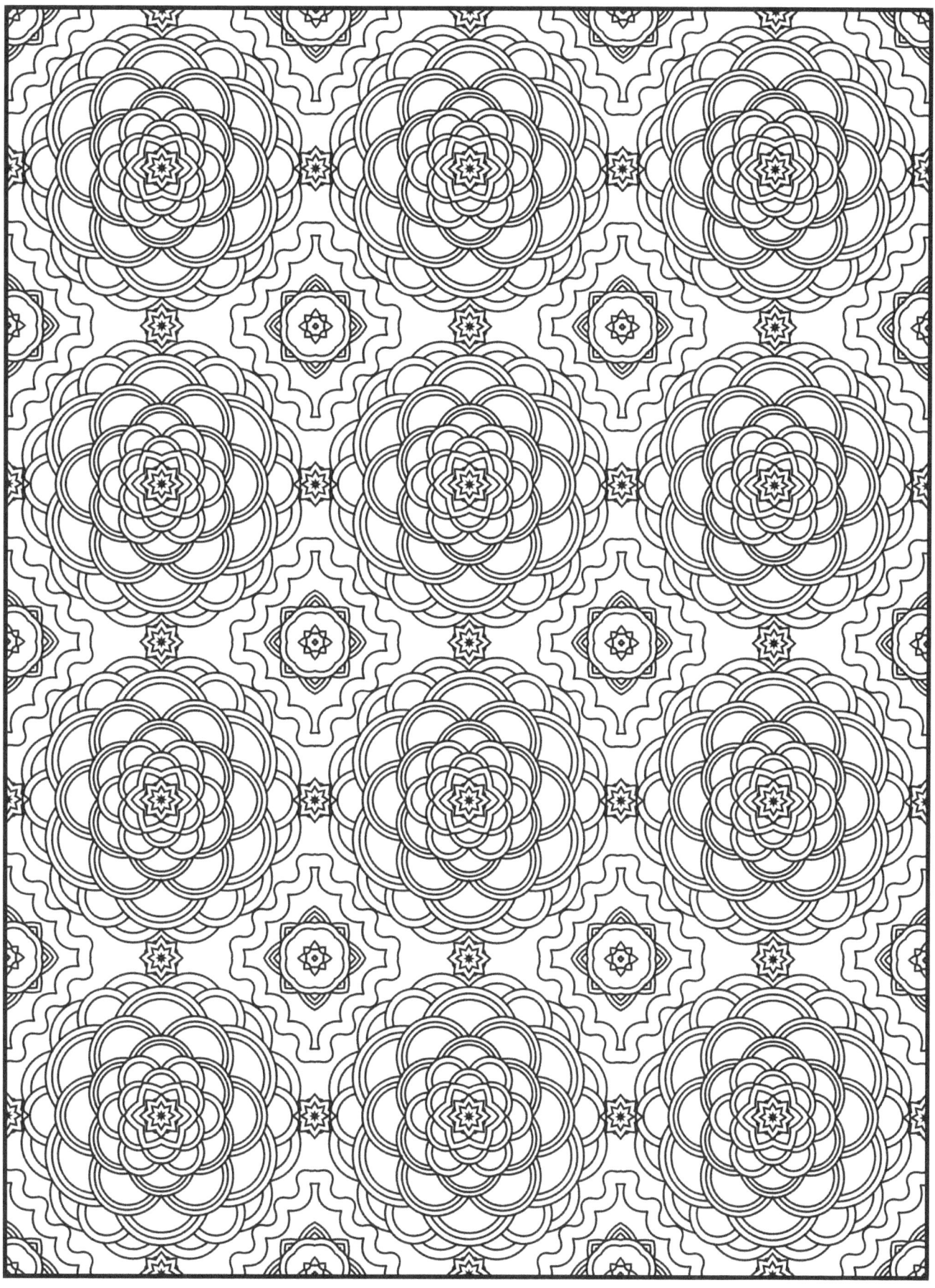

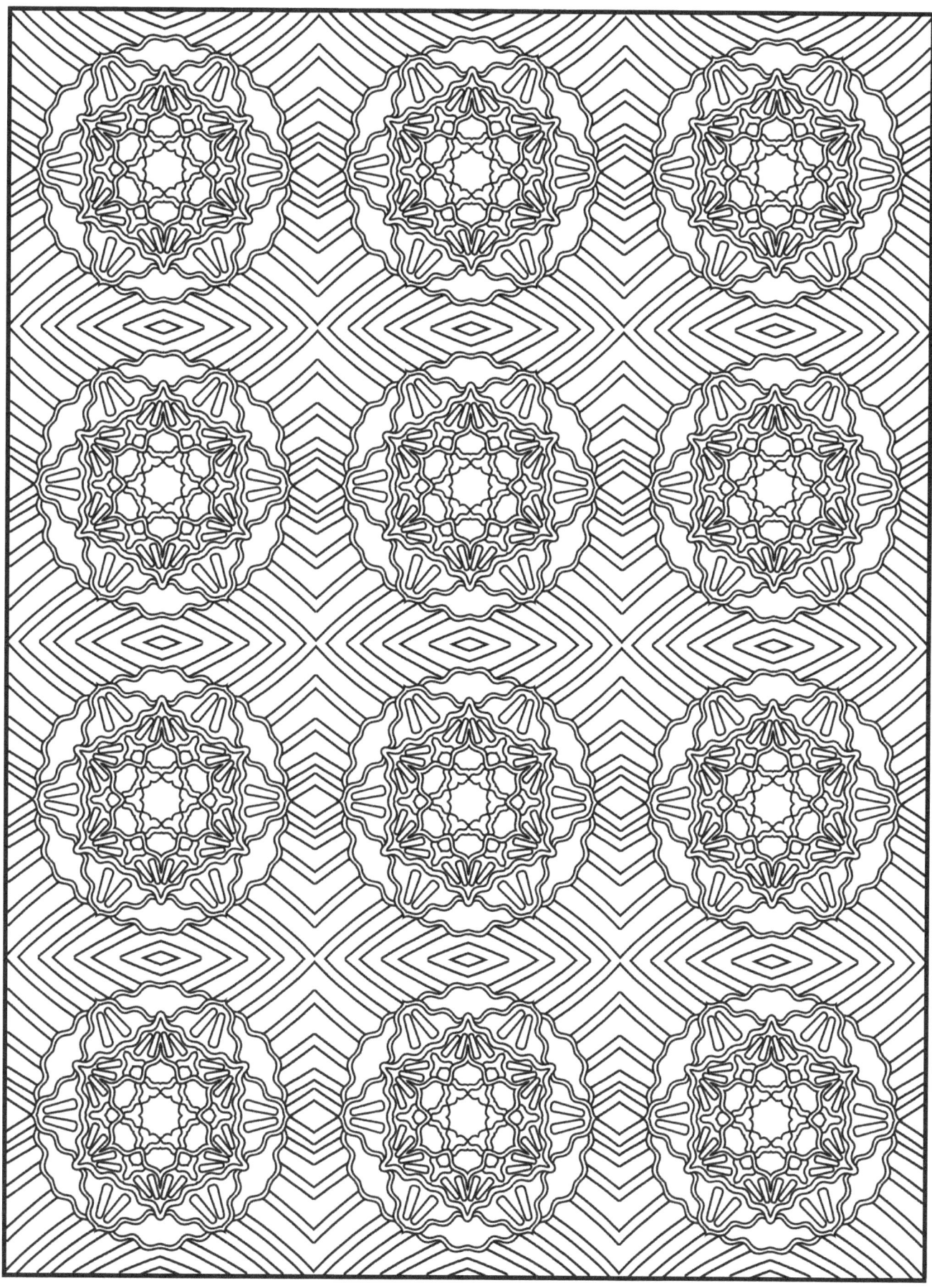

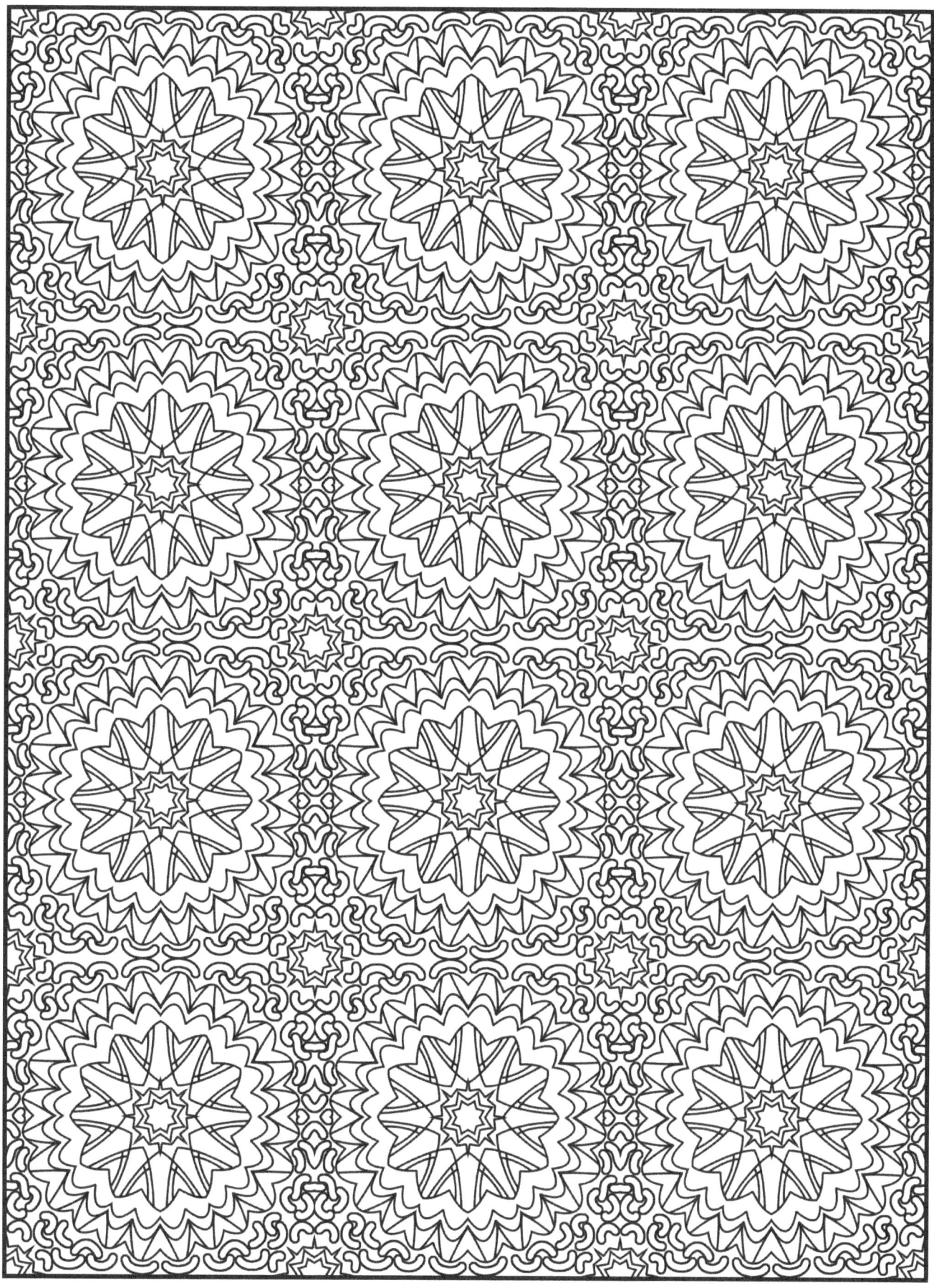

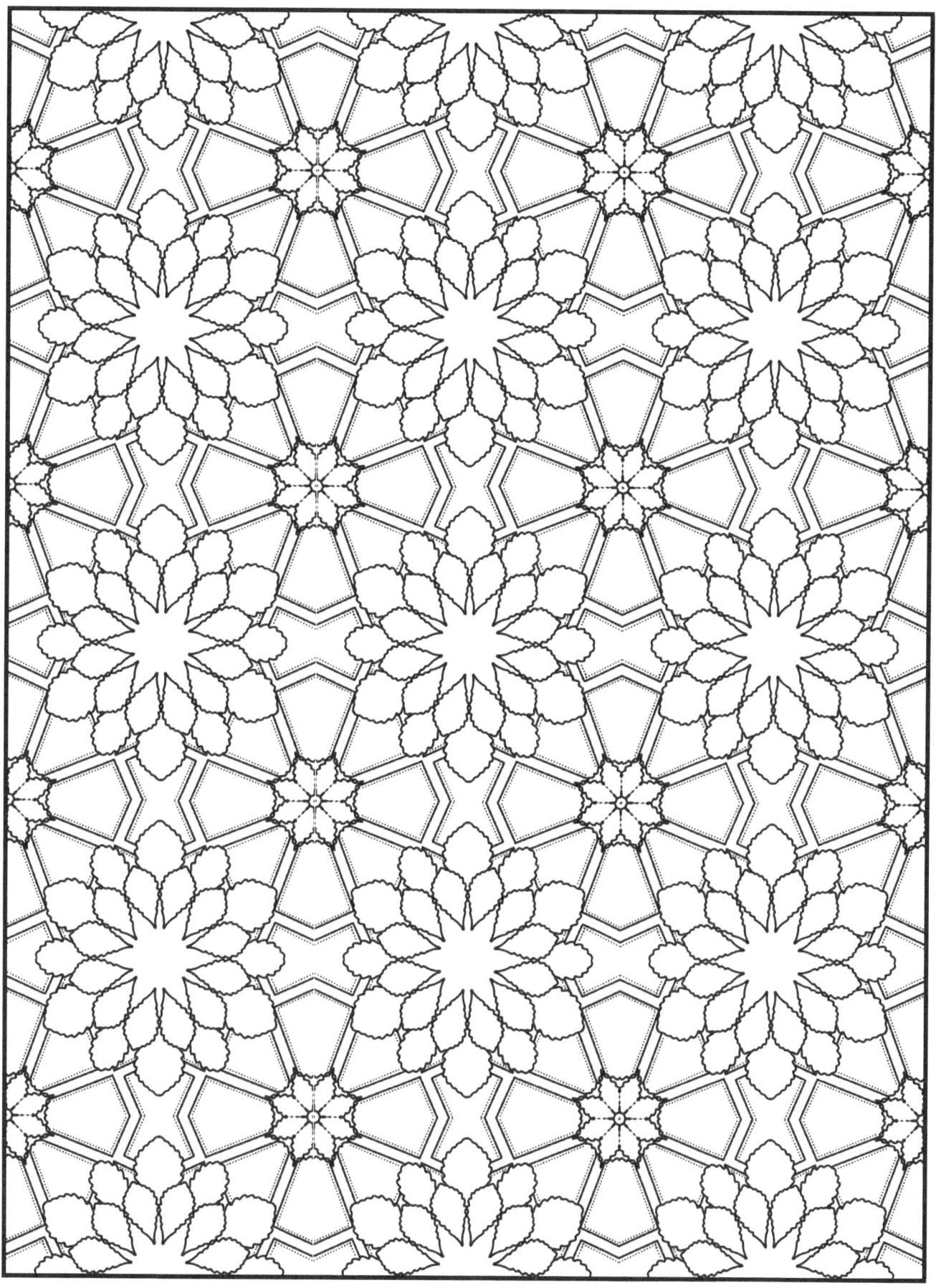

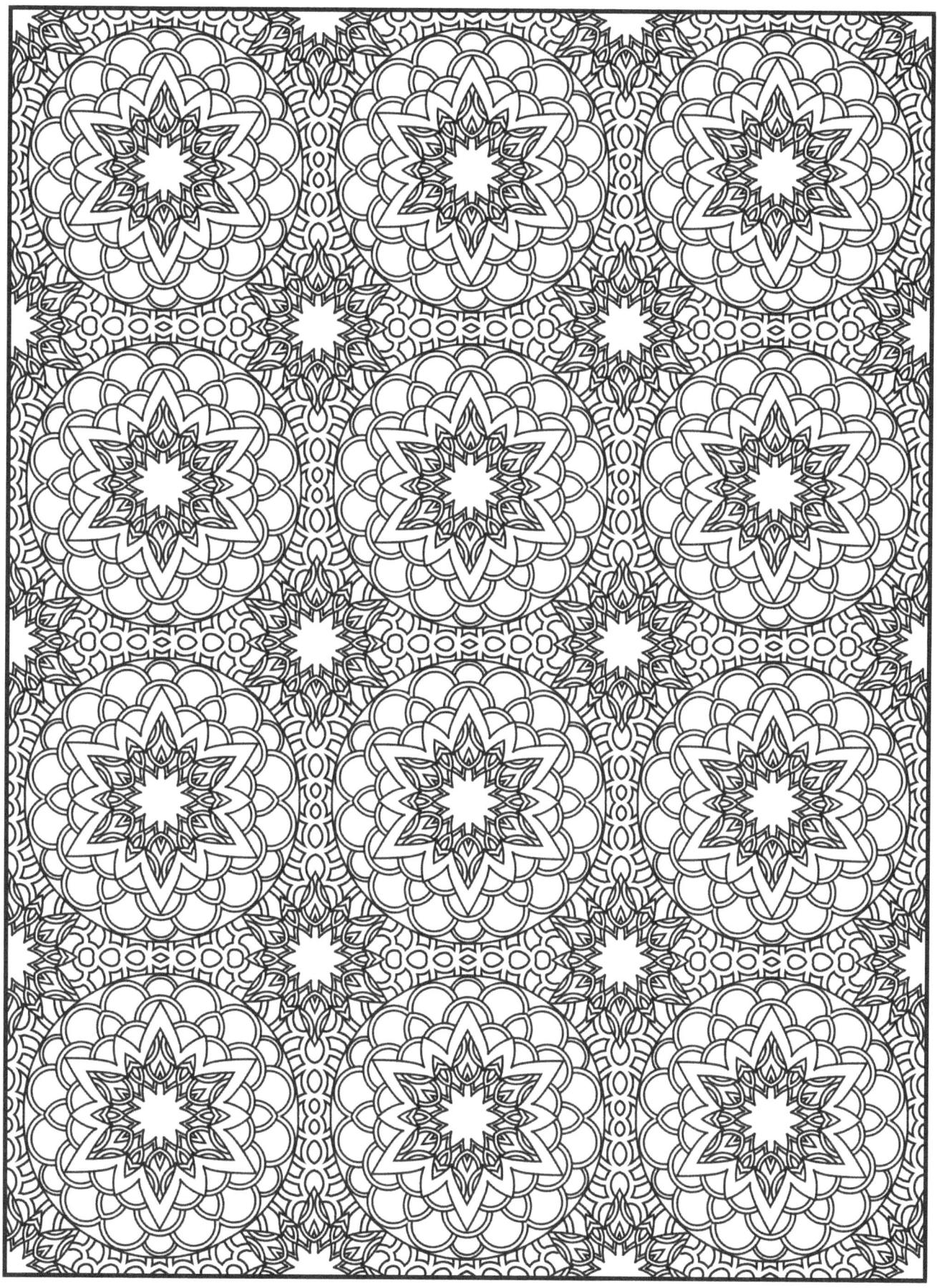

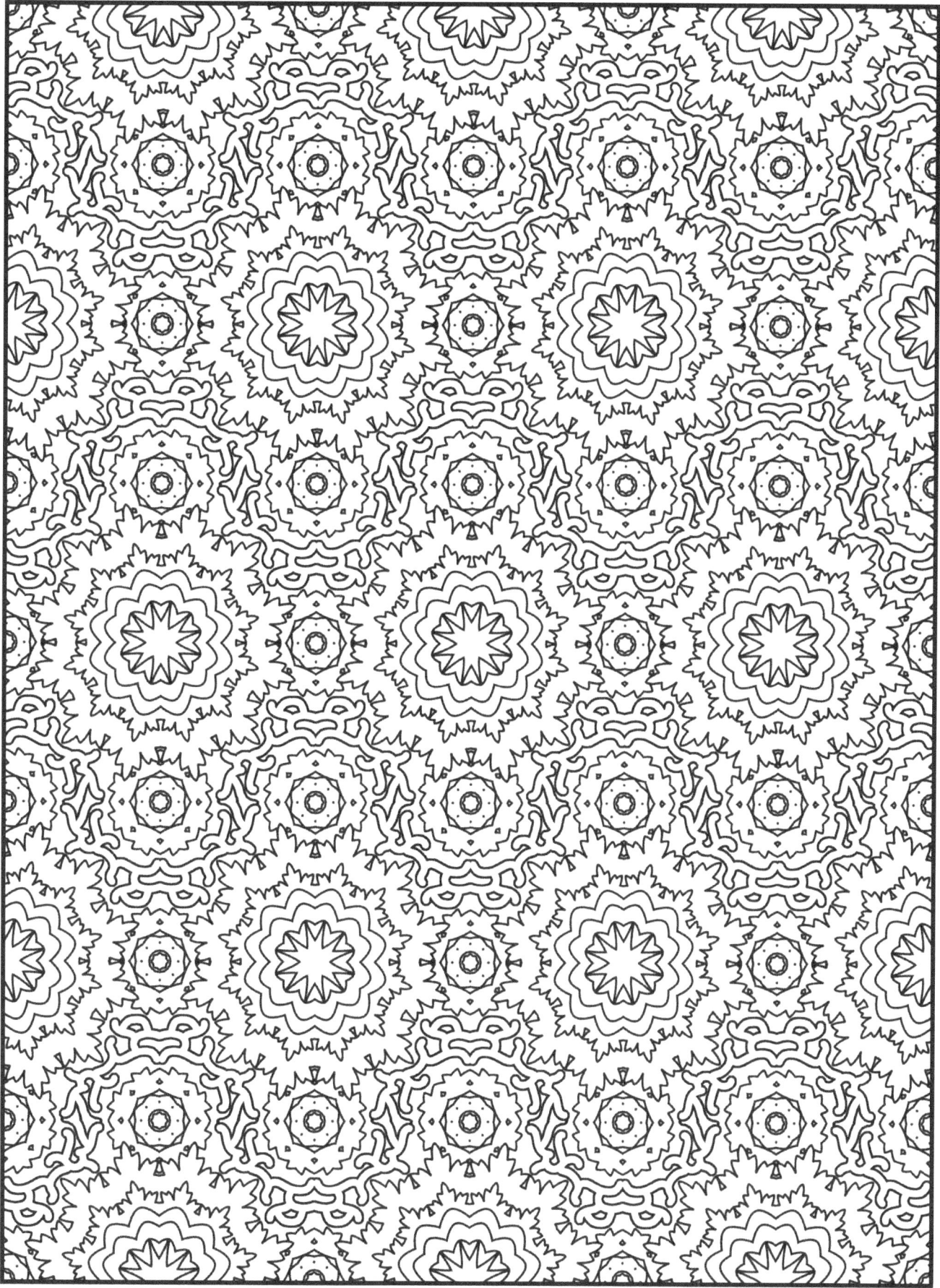

OTHER COLORING BOOKS
FROM IRONPOWER PUBLISHING

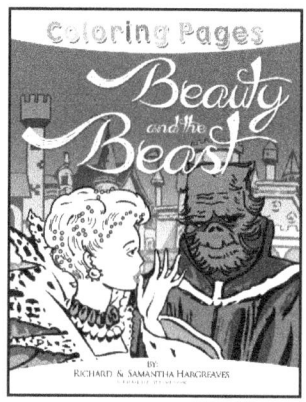 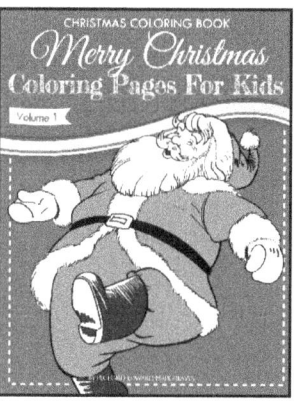 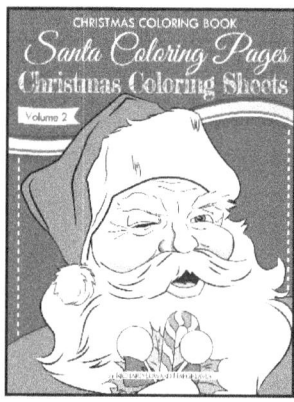 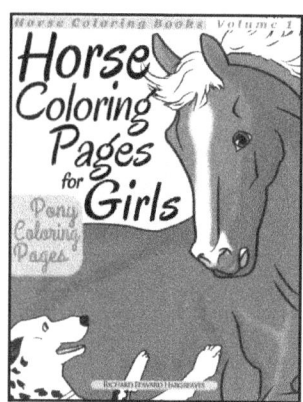

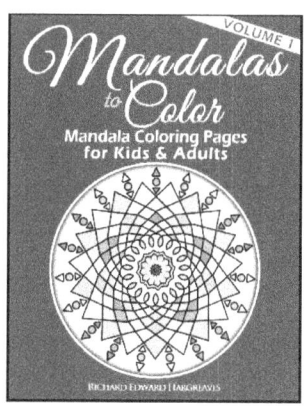 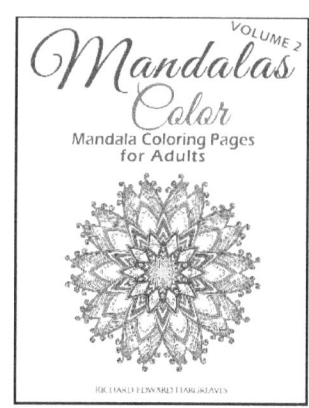 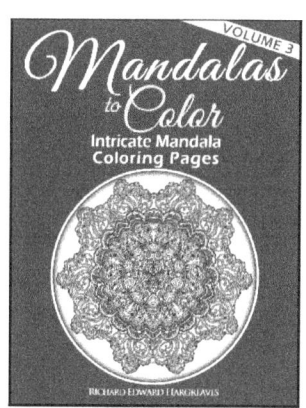

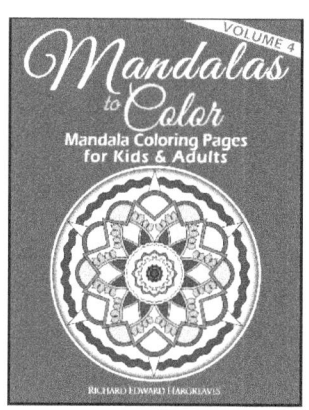 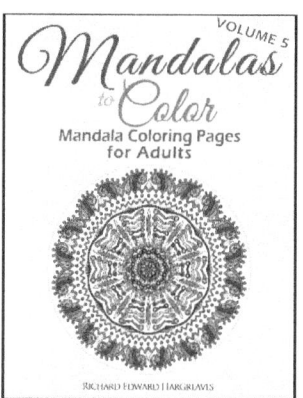 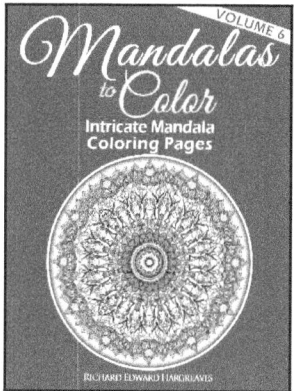 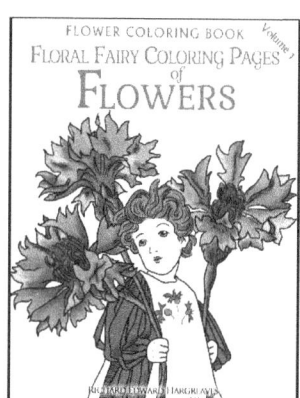